BREATH *of the* ABSOLUTE

BREATH *of the* ABSOLUTE

DIALOGUES WITH MOOJI

THE MANIFEST AND UNMANIFEST ARE ONE

Edited by
Manjusri and Zenji

Yogi Impressions®

Yogi Impressions®

BREATH OF THE ABSOLUTE
First published in India in 2010 by
Yogi Impressions Books Pvt. Ltd.
1711, Centre 1, World Trade Centre,
Cuffe Parade, Mumbai 400 005, India.
Website: www.yogiimpressions.com

First Edition, January 2010

Cover illustrations and drawings by Mooji
Cover design: Jyoti Graziano, Priya Mehta

ISBN 978-81-88479-61-0

Printed at: Thomson Press, Mumbai

You don't have to understand.
Something is moving deeper
than usual understanding.

This is the presence of Grace itself.
No one can understand Grace.
You can only say:
"Thank you. Thank you. Thank you that you've
picked me up, and that you burn me!"

Camphor burns; it leaves no residue.
This burning too will leave no residue.

[*Silence*]

The prayer is: Don't leave anything unburnt.

The ultimate state
of Supreme liberation
is one's own real nature.

It is always attained.

Knowing this, be still.

~ *Sri Ramana Maharshi*

Bhagavan Sri Ramana Maharshi

The Sage of Arunachala
Guru of Sri Poonja

You are the One
which is aware of the awareness
of objects and ideas.

You are the One
which is even more silent
than awareness.

You are the Life
which precedes
the concept of life.

Your nature is Silence
and it is not attainable,

It always Is.

~ Papaji

Sri Harilal Poonja

Beloved 'Papaji'

Prostrations at the feet of my Master

the embodiment of grace, wisdom and love
the light of whose presence
dispels all doubts and delusion
thus establishing the mind in its original state
– unborn Awareness

CONTENTS

Preface xiii

Introduction xvii

Advaita – The Pathless Path 3

The Time Bomb Is Ticking 11

The Master Key 15

When the Self Is Seen 19

You Are Perfect as You Are 25

You Must Taste This! 29

Ambassador to Freedom 37

Power-Cut to the Mind 41

Delusion of Consciousness 45

'And then . . .' 51

Let the Sleeping Bag 'I' Unzip 57

The Seed 'I Am' 61

Subtler than Space 65

An Appointment with the Buddha 71

Being Honey 75

When Pain and Peace Are One 81

Caviar of the Beingness 85

The Original Being 91

Hiding in the Pillow of God 95

Removing the Cataract of 'I' 101

Wherever I Am, I Am Still 105

Being the One Without History 109

Lingo of Oneness 115

Giving Up the Firm 121

The 'I' Is Called into the Witness Box 125

Take a Look at the Observer 131

Untouchable 137

Amnesia in the Beingness 141

Dead on Arrival 149

Pregnant with Your Self 153

Being Asleep While Fully Awake 159

Satsang Is the Mirror of the Self 165

Seeing from Freedom 171

My Final Question 175

Breath of the Absolute 181

Who Is Mooji? 185

A Note on Arunachala 205

Acknowledgements 207

PREFACE

The editors prostrate themselves in front of this
incredible Power that is the Truth,
which they have come to know through Mooji,
whom they regard as this same eternal Truth
that never comes and goes,
ever reliably and accessibly shining
in the Heart of all!

For as far back as memory can reach, before Mooji came along, life was viewed as nothing but the sum total of mind-based and bodily experiences. The self in our minds was defined as equal to the circumference of the physical body. Experience after experience was strung together to form a unique biography. Some episodes of this accumulated history in our lives were pleasurable and impelled us to beg for encores, while others were so unpleasant that they were banned into the darkness of the unconscious, decreed never to see the light of day again – as if it were really possible.

This attitude wasn't unique to us, rather it is endemic, and is borne out of innocent ignorance. Approaching life like this may appear wise at some point in time, but, as Mooji shows, it has a dramatic and adverse impact on the quality of our lives, both inside the body and the way the external is further experienced. Humanity's habit of looking towards and managing experiences has a direct relationship with the suffering humankind endures. This strategy of screening the experiential realm for good versus evil, so as to select the agreeable or to manipulate anything that isn't perceived as desirable has, over time, brought about a sculpted image of ourselves as a person. The sense of 'I' as an individual encased in a physical body is an idea which we started to believe in and identify with, and we can't even remember when it all began. This watchlist of desirable and undesirable experiences, along with the idea of the one holding this list, acts like a roll of film through which the Power and Light of the Consciousness projects itself and thus appears our world with us as a moving part in it. Much like a movie or a dream, this world – as Shakespeare so wisely indicated – is a stage; a grand and intimate stage, where we as independent actors act out lives we know and call our own. With constant reinforcement, the way in which we experience ourselves continues to appear convincingly real up until we start questioning it.

This book has the purpose, if ever there is one, to sow the seed for you to start questioning your assumptions about yourself and life; and also to encourage whatever of this natural inclination is already showing itself in you to come to full bloom and to bring about the ultimate result, which is the realisation that you are one with this Truth Mooji is pointing towards.

Each chapter is based on a dialogue that unfolded during satsangs that Mooji has held over the past several years at the foot of the holy mountain, Arunachala. Bhagavan Sri Ramana Maharshi, who regarded and adored Arunachala as his own Sadguru, is himself the Guru of Mooji's Master, the much revered Sri H.W.L. Poonja – lovingly referred to as Papaji by his own devotees and by many sincere seekers of Truth who have met Papaji through Mooji's presence.

We offer these pages to this Truth we love, in thanks and joy for all the blessings that we have received. By merely drinking from the well-spring of the Source-Consciousness, out of which Mooji's words emanate, we are continuously and consistently, with undeniable potency and precision, pointed back to ourselves as formless Reality.

Our gratefulness to Mooji knows no bounds for having entrusted us with his words, for giving us the privilege to contemplate his utterances so that we could make the Truth, as spoken through him, suitable for print. This work feels to us like entering our Master's sacred Heart Chamber, and we love it so.

May this book bear fruit in you, most beloved reader, by inspiring you to ponder without thinking what is being shared inside each chapter, so that this Truth that already Is may kiss you from inside and unveil itself as the formless Presence forever radiant, in which and by which your form and the entire universe dances.

The Editors

INTRODUCTION

Breath of the Absolute is a collection of dialogues between Mooji and sincere seekers of Truth that took place in the winters of recent years at Arunachala, the sacred hill near the South Indian town of Tiruvannamalai.

The subject of any of Mooji's talks, and so this book is no exception, is your own Self. Like a warm-hearted, loving parent he uses words like a bar of soap to rub off false beliefs and assumptions that have kept us imprisoned in a world of our own making. Before we take Mooji at his word and investigate what we believe we know, we may not have even realised that we are the creators of our own suffering. This is not to say that the search for Truth has any goal other than Its own recognition.

Mooji points out the following: We exist; each and every one of us already knows this as a fact. But what is new and fresh is his invitation that we entertain this poignant question: As what do we exist?

Even when this question has started to excite us, our proclivity to listen to and believe in mind keeps us still thinking that it is up to us to create and achieve our Self.

Who we are in Truth requires nothing to be revealed to us except our willingness to look and to question the familiar suggestions of mind. The discovery is immediate, and no prior knowledge of any kind is needed. In fact, it is due to acquired knowledge and our belief in it that this simple Truth of our existence appears to us as obscured and inaccessible.

Mooji discourages you from reading this book as if it were a textbook for study. He does not trust learning as a means for you to realise the Truth. The focus of his words of wisdom you find printed in these pages is entirely on arousing in you the determination to carry out and follow through with the investigation that is suggested. Hence, this publication is not to be read from cover to cover or even in sequential order. Go to any chapter that attracts you and read it paragraph by paragraph. Don't abide by convention that would have you read through an entire chapter all at once. The main purpose is for you to contemplate in your own heart what is being shared with you, without turning any of it into homework. This approach is supported by the brevity of the chapters that are also self-contained and arranged without any particular order. Thus, the presentation of the material does not assume any progression.

Keep in mind that Mooji's advice is directed towards the Consciousness. So, leave it up to the Consciousness to carry it out. If the questions and the directions given are not embraced with joy in the heart, then this is a clear sign that mind is engaged. When this happens, it does not mean that you are failing. Don't buy into any suggestion of success or failure, both of which are nothing but ideas arising in and as mind. As Mooji would say, you are still here, present as the uninvolved and neutral Observer of the apparent success or failure.

Don't give up! Initially, it may feel like you are in the middle of an arm-wrestling match. But, eventually your determination to stay the course will have the mind surrender, and the Truth that's always been here will most certainly reveal itself again to you as you. How could it not? Mooji's main message is that you are and have always been the Self, even if it still awaits recognition in you!

Although we said that no prior knowledge is required, Mooji does of course use concepts to direct you to your own Self beyond any concept. This may appear to you as a contradiction. Terms such as the Absolute, Awareness, Consciousness, Existence, Self and Truth are frequently employed to point you Home. The experience of the editors has been that none of these words need any definition to be understood. There is a capacity alive in us that knows how to make use of Mooji's concepts. The Consciousness will in time fill in more and more the true meaning by way of your own Self-discovery, even though we must stress once again that it is not a prerequisite for Self-knowledge to emerge in Its completeness.

These pointers are not rigid frameworks containing the Truth. Truth has no structure and cannot be confined by any concept. It is formless, beyond and at the same time prior to any mental understanding. Words which emanate directly from this Source – through one who is liberated from the ego – have life and power of their own. An energetic transmission of the Truth rather than a mental comprehension occurs. So listen not to preconceived meanings that the words carry for you, instead listen to where these words are coming from and where they are received in you, for this is where they are pointing.

Likewise, Mooji stresses again and again that he is speaking as pure Consciousness to pure Consciousness. This is true even when references are made to the relative plane of existence, such as 'effort' and 'responsibility'. The Consciousness 'I Am' is like a sliding bar where at one end 'I Am' is the pure, untouched, immaculate Consciousness, unidentified with any perceived objects in manifestation and at the other end is the same Consciousness lost in the identification of its own projections – the egoic mind (*see* Chapter 'Being Asleep While Fully Awake'). At any point along this bar, the 'I Am' can be addressed. Being the underlying non-dual substratum of manifestation, all is contained within and emanates out of It, therefore the one being spoken to is always Consciousness itself.

A note from the editors on variations in spelling of certain concepts: The meaning of a given term is identical whether it is capitalised or not. For added distinction we capitalise a term when it points directly to the highest understanding of our non-dual Nature or Unicity of Being, whereas its lowercase variant refers to its conventional usage. However, this differentiation should not distract you from the main message. No such differences are conveyed when Mooji speaks and still the same benefit is reaped.

We now invite you to rest your full attention on Mooji and your own Self!

The Editors

ADVAITA – THE PATHLESS PATH

Your own Master, Papaji, is often called an Advaita master. Sri Ramana Maharshi, who is Papaji's Guru, is credited by many for having enlivened this ancient non-dual philosophy in modern times. May I ask you then, what is Advaita all about?

Advaita is about You; about who or what you are. The great appeal of Advaita is that you don't need any religious background. You don't need to believe in anything at all. People from all backgrounds come to Advaita and are welcomed. A longing inside the heart to know yourself or to be free of suffering must be there for anyone to realise the Truth of what this ancient and practical philosophy is pointing towards.

Advaita is direct in that it points to the Truth immediately, from the very first moment. First it points out that you are complete as you are; then it begins to guide you out of suffering.

There is no path. This is the ultimate Truth. As this understanding deepens, a great unburdening unfolds. Here you are not being told that you must be fit for this journey; that you must meditate daily; be committed or be strong. All that this sort of advice does is put tasks in front of you before

3

you have even begun your enquiry. The absence of any spiritual practice in Advaita is the main difference when compared with many other paths that start with the assumption that you are your mind, that you are bound and that you have to do something to become free. Advaita shows you right from the beginning that who you really are has always been free. You are being pointed directly towards the ever-perfect and unchanging reality of Being – your core Self. First, discover Truth, then do whatever pleases your heart.

There is actually a lot of freedom in Advaita then.

There is not just a lot of freedom, there is *total* Freedom. Why? Because Advaita is pointing out that Freedom is not something you can earn. Freedom is what you are.

So in that Freedom, how are emotions looked upon and handled?

Emotions are only the expression of the universal Being. Everything, not only emotions but every action, every thought, every movement; all is included in this marvellous expression of the Beingness. Advaita does not focus on interpreting any particular movement. Little attention or importance is put on this 'play of waves'. Emotions are given room to express, to exhaust their expression and find peace again inside the Being.

The presence and play of emotions are not a measure of the pure Awareness you are. The one who has awakened to the Truth, is no longer identified with any object, thought, person or emotion. They do not suffer any disappointment for they are free from expectations. They are one with the natural flow of manifestation, with the natural dance of the cosmic energy as it appears in these bodies. Although conditioning may still manifest, there is no inner association with that. Thus, they remain naturally free. Without identifying with personal memory, all the noise of conditioning dissolves. The very concept of conditioning, itself recognised as mere thought, gradually fades away in time.

My background is yoga and meditation. To be in satsang and to read about Advaita confuses me somehow.

This is natural. The mind is confused, because mind is always trying to get, to understand, to have the feeling 'I know this', 'I understand this', 'I know where I am going'. The mind is very much on a linear, progressive projection. So, initially, when it is hit by something as simple as non-duality, where there is nowhere for it to 'go', nothing for it to 'grasp', the conditioned mind will get very confused, very confused indeed.

So, it is actually quite simple.

It is even simpler than simple. Simple implies that there is something you need to do that is not difficult, but This exists before even the idea of it being simple is thought of. It is experienced as difficult because you cannot get the notion out of your mind that you are bound.

Countless concepts are picked up by the mind, and in clinging to those untruths we suffocate our spontaneity, the recognition of our inherent Being. So it is the mind that says, 'I don't understand!' How can the mind understand total simplicity when its nature is to make complex what is already natural?

What is self-enquiry?

Self-enquiry is the mirror in which the Eternal recognises itself. By looking with the aid of this mirror, you come to know instantaneously who you really are; not who your body is, not who you think you are or who others say you are; no, through this looking a direct non-dual perception of your Self is revealed.

Your Self is not an object, how can the mind find or reach that which is not an object? I don't just mean physical objects. A thought is as much an object of perception as any material thing is, and so are feelings, images, memories and sensations. In short, all phenomena are objects. Mind is accustomed to interpreting and measuring phenomena. So how can the mind discover that which is aware of phenomena, which is your own Self – the one Reality?

You are aware of anything that appears in front of you on the screen of Consciousness. Where is the world without you? Where and what are thoughts without you, the perceiver of them? Where are experiences without you, the one who perceives them? You are the root and source of every experience. There cannot be any experience without you.

I've been told that Advaita Vedanta is the highest spiritual teaching.

Really and truly, Advaita is not a teaching. I would not call it a teaching. A teaching requires someone who will study and learn. Advaita goes straight in and asks, "Who is it that is going to learn? Can you learn to be you?"

More and more people, I think, are searching for freedom.

To be honest, I once believed the same, but then I saw that most people are searching for fulfilment of their projections. That really they are inside their minds and the mind only pretends to want freedom. In fact, the mind does not want Freedom at all. It is the last thing it wants because Freedom kills the conditioned mind. But yes, there is a growing attraction towards spiritual discovery. This is a good thing, even if initially one starts in a roundabout way. You're on the boat. You might change from a raft and get onto a hovercraft and next move onto a ship, but it is still good – although you are not *in* the water, at least you're *on* the water. But I don't care for all the excitement about this big shift in universal Consciousness being underway, because there is a lot of misunderstanding of what Truth actually means and Is. For Truth you have to leave aside and undress yourself of all your projections, conditioning and concepts, and then when you are completely undressed, you don't pick up new ones, you remain naked.

Can Advaita help make a better world?

When you are free from the hypnotic influence of your own concepts, your mind's conditioning and vain projections, then you are truly available to your own Self. There will not be any internal restrictive energy or any need to manipulate others to satisfy your projections. Somehow, your environment is automatically uplifted by your presence. Just like trees provide us with the oxygen to breathe, for which nobody is thanking them, human beings who have awakened to Truth radiate deep peace, communion and love without making any conscious effort to do so. Peace is their very nature. There is a saying that, 'If I have a loaf of bread and I give you half, I have half left, but if I give you all of my knowledge and love, I still have all of my knowledge and all of my love left.' And this is what the sharing of Truth is. You're not sharing objects, it is a sharing of the Subject, and the Subject cannot be divided. You are That.

So to answer your question, can Advaita, which means the true understanding and experience of Truth, help the world? Of course it can! Even with your very seeking for Truth, you are not only helping yourself but other beings are helped automatically, as well. When your mind is turned towards Righteousness, towards Peace, simultaneously there will be the quest to remove hatred, fear and desire, which are all forms of ignorance. Your search is holy because you turn your face towards Truth and people are drawn to this Truth, which is another name for who we are.

A starving man
is not 'interested' in food,
nor is a drowning man
'interested' in air.

For one longing for Liberation
Self-knowledge is not an interest.

It is vital.

THE TIME BOMB
IS TICKING

That which you are is so simple – simpler than simple even. Confirm this for yourself and know it deeply. This will put an end to all suffering and nonsense. You can do it! I know this from my own experience. It is my own discovery I'm sharing with you. That is why I cannot send you the long way Home. The discovery of your own Self is direct and instantaneous, and this is what I'm showing you. Don't waste any time. Find out, what is the essence of that which you call yourself? When you boil it down, what are you looking at?

For myself, I found that looking like this, not only did it require no incredible discipline, but most importantly it revealed that there is no distance to cover to be and to know the Self.

Just an urge must be inside of you to find this out. You are not even responsible for that. It is like a time bomb ticking away. This time bomb is set off by your exposure to the Truth being shared with you here. Not everyone is able or willing to look directly at who they are by questioning the most cherished of assumptions: 'I'.

How paradoxical, that finding out who you are in truth seems so hard. The mind can invent such an incredible delusion — incredible illusion, incredible delusion. How else is one to explain why That which is the most obvious is so obviously missed?

THE MASTER KEY

I just feel there must be something deeper that is independent of all moods and of everything that happens!

There is a contentment which is not at all affected by the surface play in the mind, the emotions or any sensation, no matter how gross or subtle. This contentment is not 'about' something, and so it is impossible for anything to have any power over it. It is Self-content, Self-radiant, Self-complete. Absorbed in the Bliss of its own existence, it does not reach for 'other' to fulfil itself.

From this Contentment the whole universe arises and plays. Part of that play is the dissatisfaction you are feeling with the ephemeral quality of ego-based pleasure, the constant fluctuation of emotional highs and lows, this unstable realm of interrelated opposites as well as the phenomena themselves.

Everybody has experienced peace at some time or other, but it never remained. Whilst identified as an entity which is subject to these passing states, there is an obvious preference for states which are experienced as peace and happiness and the avoidance of those which are not so pleasant, you see?

We put so much energy to keep the wheel of positive thinking, of self-progress, of self-understanding, of self-improvement turning, believing that somehow with all this effort we can achieve and perpetuate a stable realm of joy. It takes an enormous amount of resources of mind and body to keep the momentum going. And if you rest for only a short time, then it starts to regress, and you are forced to pick it up again and spin onwards. Around and around it goes. With your vision continually set on some imaginary point in the future, or an ideal in the mind of where it will end; both of which are impossible to reach.

This one, who is pedalling the wheel, who is practising and improving, who is enthusiastic at times, at other times not, sometimes very happy and positive about life, sometimes feeling depressed, even suicidal; this one, I would like to meet. The one who longs for a deeper level of contentment, the seeker of the happiness untouched by sorrow, let us meet this one, today! The one who says, 'In spite of so many years of practice, I have not attained that state of effortless equilibrium.' Can you find this one?

This question is the master key!

I believe there is power in Ramana's cave . . .

There is power in your own cave.
You have to sit inside the cave of your own Heart.
Ramana is also there.

WHEN THE SELF IS SEEN

Sri Ramana Maharshi says that when you abide in the Self, the Self is seen, and the world is not seen. When the world is seen, the Self is not seen. I definitely see the world, so how can you insist, then, that the Self is always here?

This is a beautiful and an excellent question, because for as long as this remains unresolved for you, some fear will lurk in the background to molest you with doubts like these: 'Who wants to be the Self, even if it's beautiful, if there's no world?' or 'If I fully realise my Self, my family won't exist anymore. Do I want to take this risk?'

To tackle this question, let's begin as follows. In order to perceive the world, there must be an interested perceiver. You believe that all of us see the same world. But this is not true. Actually, each one of us perceives a world that is one-of-a-kind. In each body-mind mechanism, a unique dreaming takes place. What do I mean by dreaming? By that I mean that you don't see the world really as it is. You see the world as your conditioning allows you to perceive it. Let me give you a simple example from ordinary life. If you've got a

Volkswagen Beetle, and you love this car, then, if there's another one in town, you're going to notice it immediately. It's going to be fluorescent for you. It comes into your consciousness because of your interest. Before this interest developed for you, you didn't pay this type of car any attention at all. You wouldn't have seen this type of car even if it had passed you by a million times. I'm sure you know this. This illustrates your tendency to see what you desire to see. You see what your conditioning and your attention directs you towards.

When you investigate the one who's interested in a life in the world and you find out that that one is just as much a perceived phenomenon as the 'world' is, somehow through this discovery the Self is revealed. Where are your attachments in that moment of recognition? Where is your desire? Where are your fears? Where is your self-interest? Everything is blown away.

The senses are still functioning, the images of the world are still there; but the attachments and the fears are gone, because the one who would experience them disappeared. You are now in the Self. This is what Bhagavan means when he says, 'When you are the Self, the world is not seen'.

Sri Ramana is also known for this wonderful utterance:

> *The Self alone is real*
> *The world is not real*
> *The Self is the world*

This rounds it up beautifully, because here Sri Ramana confirms that the material manifestation, which is innocent in itself, does not disappear; only the one who has created a personal relationship with what is seen, drops away. When this happens, the world is seen as it is.

There's a saying,

I am not seeing the world as it is
I am seeing the world as I am

This means that the world as you see it reflects who you think you are. For as long as you purchase your conditioning as having something to do with you, you are dreaming a dream of separation in which you experience yourself as an autonomous player in the world you love and don't want to let go of. When it is recognised that both the conditioning and the apparent one who is conditioned are ideas arising in unconditioned Being – the Self – this dream ends, with Silence, Beauty and Peace being revealed unto itself. This is your immediate experience. This is your direct experience. It takes no time!

[*Silence*]

The essential thing is to be clear about what you are,
by being clear about what you are not.
When this door of recognition opens,
Grace enters.

YOU ARE PERFECT AS YOU ARE

I had this experience of dropping into the heart and the mind stopped.
Is that what you mean by 'being quiet'?

It is to be quiet to the point where you don't even know
who is being quiet! Only quiet is left, no 'you' being quiet.
When only quiet is left, 'I am quiet' will not be there.
Everything comes into Silence.

Mind has a lot of trouble with this kind of exploration,
this kind of discovery, because it cannot be proud of it.
You are returning home to your own Buddha-Nature, your
own Christ-Consciousness – into total Silence. This Silence
cannot be acquired and cannot be grasped, because there
is nothing apart from It to achieve It. You are That!

Sometimes it feels like the little 'me' is under attack.

The thought of yourself is under attack from other thoughts,
all generated from your mind. That Stillness, the mind can do
nothing to or about, because It cannot be added onto nor taken
away from. Beyond the possibility and concept of attack,

the Stillness does not need to be defended or to be defended against. It is perfect as it Is. You are perfect as you Are. Only when you have cleaned yourself of all that is not you, will you lose the fear of Existence; then you will dance as Existence itself.

There is the image of Atlas, this figure crouched over with the world on top of his back. Another figure is dancing on top of the world, Nataraj! Two sides of one expression. Either you can carry the world weighted on your head or you dance.

You are Nataraj or Atlas. You choose.

There are some of you here for the final time. You are not dedicated to freedom in instalments; you are going for the whole thing. A willingness is present, to simply discover with your entire being what your mind is trying to avoid. You are not creating a way to be. You are what you are and you are that now! But, you must watch for the thought giving you the sense that you still have something to do, somewhere to go. Because you accept these types of thoughts without question, your experience will be that of being separate. Then some subtle waiting occurs, but for what? Is Reality going to come from some place? The sense of waiting is prolonging the delusion of separation.

Stop creating or holding an image of yourself, an image of you is not you. It's a subtle but virile idea in the mind. Not everyone can hear these words right now or can see what they are pointing to.

All of them are pointing to you! There is nothing you need to do to Be.

YOU MUST TASTE THIS!

There must be some desire for you to pick up self-enquiry and carry it out. I ask you why do you want to know anything at all?

Because there's still a trace of 'I', and living as an 'I' causes dissatisfaction.

Did you find this out yourself or did you learn this?

This is what I feel.

Okay, so what you feel is that as long as there is 'I', there is dissatisfaction. For whom is the dissatisfaction?

It's the 'I' itself that represents dissatisfaction, it's a limitation.

What is making this observation that 'I' itself represents dissatisfaction? These are your words. Tell me for whom is it dissatisfying?
Now we're talking facts.

So, you say, it is observed that wherever there's 'I', dissatisfaction exists. What is complaining? Is it the 'I' or something else?

It must be the 'I'.

It must be 'I'. If the 'I' is dissatisfied, to whom will the 'I' complain? Now, that which watches this dissatisfied 'I', is that itself dissatisfied? Whether there's satisfaction or dissatisfaction, for whom are these and what observes this?

[*Silence*]

In my view, finding out to whom all experiences report is something to be clear about. Otherwise you're bound to put a lot of money and energy behind lesser questions, not realising that all you are doing is pouring your precious resources down the drain. So, check out what you are investing in and see if it is worth it.

When you ask who knows that the 'I' is dissatisfaction, immediately the answer comes: I am. With this question my attention shifts to this place of only consciousness and there everything is fine.

Slow down right now! What even watches Consciousness? Am I going too far in asking you this?

Let's recap: You have taken up the question, "Who is this 'I' that suffers dissatisfaction?" You've reported your findings: The attention moves away from the subject of the question – 'I' – and drops into that natural, intuitive sense 'I Am'.

As this happens, the discontented 'I' loses its distinction and fades into non-existence. All the experiences known to 'I' have the same fate.

Even when the personal 'I' has dissolved, still a sense of 'I' remains. This remaining 'I' is impersonal. We call it the intuition 'I Am' for the sake of clarity. In the presence of 'I Am' the disturbed 'I', the personal 'I', is seen as nothing more than thought.

My follow-up question is: Can this 'I Am' be observed?

It sounds to me like you want us to go even a step further when you ask, "Who is aware of 'I Am'?"

What I'm pointing out is something you have already declared with these words: 'I know I am'. You know that you're conscious and that you are experiencing through Consciousness. Consciousness and the functioning of Consciousness are perceivable and are perceived. Who is the perceiver of this great subtlety?

[*Silence*]

Every human being should taste this! Leave everything aside. Don't search for anything through what you think you know. Your education will not support this. Everything you have ever read and studied, leave it alone. Leave everything alone and be alone. Leave everything aside until there's something that cannot be left aside, and then speak from this place. Speak if you can find any disharmony, or lack. Know this place, this place-less place. Be confirmed there; then you can move anywhere in existence and nowhere will you be troubled. Undress yourself of all the concepts you've picked up. Have enough courage to stand entirely alone and see if any questions remain to be asked.

Can you see everything is thought? Everything is thought! Even the grandest thing is thought. Thoughts cannot exist without you. You are the witness of them; you are the purchaser of them. You are the employer of them. They report to you. Who are you? You must taste This!

The human body is a great privilege for it allows us to ask these questions. No other species has the capacity to enquire, but you have, and to find out with certitude. Out of your dissatisfaction you long for lasting satisfaction. Discover what will and does not leave you. Everything else will leave you. With the gift of this body, you have this great opportunity to discover the Truth of your Existence, but you waste it if all pursuits are merely regarding the body and fulfilment of the mind's desires! Yes, so much work we do for bodily enjoyment! But the very body that you require to enjoy, you cannot keep. Therefore, everything that you slave over in order to have a taste for five minutes, ten minutes, is washing away. What is that which cannot be washed away?

In this place I cannot even ask, 'Who am I?' or 'Who is observing this?'

Thank you! Thank you! Even these questions will not resonate, but they can come.

Ultimately, in the final seeing you recognise that whatever is perceivable is changeful, it appears in front of you and cannot be held with unbroken attention; it comes and goes. But that which observes this is what? This is not merely a mental question, so no flippant answers will do. Only those responses that arise out of pure insight will carry that lasting satisfaction. You are face to face with your own Self. You are face to face with your own Self, what do you look like?

*That which is revealed when thoughts are absent
is also here when thoughts are present.*

AMBASSADOR TO FREEDOM

The Awareness-Self that you are is not affected by activity of mind or body. Eyes open or eyes closed, it does not impact the Awareness. 'Spiritual' company does not heighten the Awareness in the same way that 'worldly' company does not diminish It. Awareness is no feeling and so It is beyond good or bad feelings. Awareness is neither personal nor impersonal, neither extraordinary nor ordinary. Awareness has no location; it makes no difference if you are at Arunachala or any place else in the world. Awareness is not at the end of some striving or practice. It cannot be divided by time or space. Your intuitive sense of 'I' is not separate from Awareness.

You are one with the Awareness when your 'I' arises without history or psychological force. You are one with the Awareness when by saying 'I' you refer to that intuition itself that is synonymous with the Beingness. If this is your position, you are not the 'I' who speaks or the 'I' who listens, neither the 'I' that doubts nor the 'I' that believes. No religion belongs to you. The roles you play in life are filled spontaneously and naturally, but you are not invested in them anymore as you used to be. You are not someone's mother. You are not someone's father. You are not someone's child or friend. Good and bad are mere words for you. No judgements are of any significance. You understand that everything that comes and goes is part of a package deal. It is nothing more than the human expression. Every sensation, every mood, every play of mind is only a wave on the surface of the ocean. How long will it take you to realise this Truth?

[*Long silence*]

Many people cannot bear this kind of talk. A rare one is undaunted by this invitation and is aroused.

I say, remove all doubts and then you in turn can be an ambassador to your own Freedom. You take this Freedom wherever you go and are the Light unto your Self.

Every human being speaks from a space of doubt, some crisis, some trouble, some worry. What is missed is that all of it is due to misidentification. It is you, the Beingness – the Absolute in manifestation – that appears to have fallen into some confusion. This confusion is the product of your own 'maya'. You have fallen under the spell, the hypnosis of your own projections and are suffering from that delusion. All that's required is a slap to awaken you – the Beingness – out of this stupor. This is what satsang is for.

You ask, "Share your knowledge with us."
I have no knowledge to share.
I do not speak from knowledge;
I speak only from Being.
I am that Being and also beyond that Being
as unknowable Awareness.

POWER-CUT TO THE MIND

Forget about all the strategies of your mind to gain knowledge and understanding. Just forget about it! Yes, forget about it! Why can't we ever forget about it?

You ask what to do to be one with Truth? I tell you the best thing to do: Take a shortcut! Forget about it! Cut the power to the mind! Lights out! This is the only strategy, if any needs to be taken, to reveal to you instantly that the eternal and timeless Freedom is already present as you!

The advice 'Forget about it!' seems totally irresponsible, even naïve, over-simplistic, but it works every time. Forget about it!

Sometimes what we share in satsang gets the mind navigating to get a grip on the subject. I say: Throw it out! Forget about it! And still, you're here, totally here, empty, without strategies. Be strategy-less and empty of intention. Like this, all things happen beautifully.

Life – the way you know it – teaches you how to walk with crutches and yet you're completely healthy. Throw away your crutches and dance! What are the crutches you depend on? Notions such as 'I am not free' or 'I'm bound by my circumstances and conditioning'.

Use your Heart, not your head! Put your Heart in front of me when you ask a question! We don't want to see your face nor your hands nor your head. Yes, not even your head I want. Speak and act from that Heart place!

Come in front of me and show me your Heart!

DELUSION OF CONSCIOUSNESS

Control is an obsession of Consciousness when it identifies. Identification with the body makes the Consciousness feel vulnerable. It knows that the body is impermanent, that it can be injured and is subject to pain, sickness and ageing; therefore, in identifying as the body, Consciousness also feels that it can be harmed or die. Furthermore, when Consciousness identifies with mind, a transfer of responsibility seems to occur. What is naturally being taken care of by Consciousness, for example: the body's welfare, comfort, actions and situations, now feels to be the duty for the limited mind to carry out all by itself. This is how Consciousness ends up experiencing guilt, shame, remorse and anxiety. It worries about doing the wrong thing, fears making a 'bad' choice or losing something that allays this constant underlying anxiety of vulnerability, or fantasises about something that will alleviate it. The mind's perception of life is wound around battling these bodily factors, and as long as the Consciousness is identified, It, too, appears immersed in this struggle.

You, the Consciousness, need this body to continue tasting and experiencing, but it is not necessary to identify with it.

Without identification, the body will still be there, and this obsession with control will fade.

The body is completely innocent in all of this. By divine decree it's there doing its work. The body doesn't know it's you. Something inside is constantly holding the body as 'me' and giving a name to it.

The mind must have something to threaten you with to hold you hostage. There must be something you want or don't want for the mind to get you to listen to its false warnings, such as 'If you don't do this, something unpleasant is going to happen.' More often than not there is the fear of change, because mind imagines what it doesn't know, or has not projected, is going to be negative. There will be a loss of some sort, or a 'stepping down' or a 'going backwards'. All of which might lead to annihilation, which is what the mind spends its whole time trying to avoid.

Be daring with life, say, "Okay, turn me into a street beggar if that is what you wish, but I'll be a free street beggar." And then you will see where the shaking is coming from. Can you do it? Others have done it, and have found when faced, their fear is but a ghost that vanishes in the light of their courage and willingness to truly see.

The fear is always greater than the actuality. The fear comes because of lack of trust. You feel you can take better care of yourself than God can. You fear what God may have planned for you may not be what you want. This is probably true because the dreams we have are confined to what we know of life and ourselves, which is infinitesimal to the vastness that Is. When we let go of what we think will make us happy, we allow Grace to breathe, and great and beautiful things not even imagined of are given space to happen.

Yet this apparent need to control, the fear of the loss of it, and the supposed breaking out of it, is also Consciousness playing because there is no individual outside of this Consciousness to decide or act contrary to the permissive will of Consciousness. Everything is Consciousness. Human beings and their activity are an effect and not the cause of Consciousness. Ponder that. Can the characters in the first chapter of a book determine how the second chapter should be? Can they command the author to change situations and characters they don't like, or prevent the next chapter from happening?

For some, seeing through the illusion of control is a deeply repressive idea while in others it's completely liberating. Consciousness is not twisting your arm. You're invited to see.

Who is aware of the search, of the seeker
and what is being sought?
Is it not you?
If what is being sought is found,
are you not there?
If it is lost,
are you not there?
Who are you?

'AND THEN . . .'

I see in many of you that you are stripped right back to Emptiness. Nobody is living behind those eyes. It is beautiful. There's space without and space within, same thing, no difference. Is it not enough? How can it be that many who have tasted their own Existence as that unchanging bliss have come to me to report the loss of this recognition? Their first words are usually 'and then . . .'. I'm curious, what is this 'and then . . .' moment? Bring me to your 'and then . . .' moment and show me what happens.

It is the identification with the body-mind that's the problem.

In this there are three factors: body, mind and identification with both. All three factors are perceivable, and you perceive them. What you call identification is some action – an attribute of Consciousness like the attention or belief – which springs out of Awareness. You say, "Identification of myself with the body-mind." My question to you is, the identification is of what with what? And who are you in this?

If you're doing your enquiry, you should be clear about it. Aren't you looking? Obviously, that which identifies with body-mind is not body-mind, is it? So if it is not body-mind, what is it? When you inspect this, you will find that both body and mind are innocent in this. There is another factor altogether responsible.

As we said at the outset, you are aware of body, mind and identification with both. Let's take a look at mind. Mind is thought. You are aware of your thoughts. Thoughts come and go. No thought is eternal. Something watches thoughts. You cannot sustain one thought unbroken. A voice says, 'Daddy' and the thought is gone. Obviously, thoughts are not permanent.

Whose thought is it? You say, "It is my thought." You don't say, "It is your thought." This 'my' must have difference in it. Look and see if this 'my' has any difference in it. Difference can only be comprised of quality. A quality is not sentient. Quality is just a phenomenon, and a phenomenon cannot recognise itself. A phenomenon is effectively an object. Something perceives the object. What is it that perceives it? Can it be different from your intuitive sense of yourself?

When you look for that which perceives the object, you will have to say, "It has to be me, I am the one who is watching all of this. I am that which watches quality." Does that which watches quality have any quality itself? If your reply is "Yes, it has quality itself" than this only means that it itself can be perceived. If it can be perceived, it is not you, the pure Observer. It is the observer mixed with some quality, a cocktail. What discerns this? When this question is engaged, something is scooping back into Infinity. It is scooping back into you. You are the Infinity. You are the one looking. What are you experiencing in the final analysis of seeing? What is left out of your research? What residue is there? This research is like lighting a block of camphor. It is going to burn, and it is not going to leave any residue. If you've done your enquiry, what remains? Who survives the enquiry?

You are the Undying, why do you think of death?
Let what is die-able die and let the Eternal be.

LET THE SLEEPING BAG 'I' UNZIP

Sometimes, in response to the penetrating power of your own satsang, a changing over of power is experienced. A shift from manual to automatic takes place. The sleeping bag 'I' unzips; the Beingness crawls out yawning and stretching as it again discovers its natural fullness. Trapped energies like your conditioning, habits, fears, attachments and desires that were once the fabric holding your sense of an independent and autonomous existence together, unravel. Dormant memories and tendencies flare up for a little bit. You will be experiencing in ways that are new for you. Therefore, it is not unusual that a lot of turbulence may be present for some time. Let everything happen. Refrain from drawing any conclusions about anything you perceive. Just keep quiet. Let it happen. Resist the tendency to interpret the events. Don't judge anything.

For a while, you may find that your life's routine is nothing like a routine anymore. You may forget your keys, your phone number, what bus to take home and so on. Panic may enter your mind. How lucky that you are in satsang, an environment where you are reminded that all of this is okay. You are held in

God's palm, so don't worry about having to take care of yourself. You have been doing that long enough. Now you are getting to know how the universe takes care of you.

Gradually, you'll feel a deeper peace inside that is not easily disturbed. Your moods will settle into a natural kind of equilibrium. It is recognised then that actions and reactions, which previously you felt deeply involved with, are perceived in this space of Awareness that you are one with, but you are not touched. There is a steadiness, a depth in this recognition, and great joy arises without reason.

The initial unsteadiness in the experiential realm represents the birth pangs as you are being reborn into Emptiness. Let that revealing happen until it stills. It is no more than the sound an empty bottle makes when you throw it into the ocean: 'blup, blup'. Once all the air is out, it becomes completely quiet and sinks to the ocean's floor. Your mind is like this bottle. At first it makes some 'blup, blup' noise until it becomes very quiet. So, don't be perturbed by these things. They will happen. Even if you think you are going nuts. This also passes. These are just little bubbles fizzing out. Resist the temptation to formulate any conclusions. It is the mind that is fighting to retain its hold. You've been living life as if you were playing it from sheet music. Now that all the paper has been burnt, you have to play your life's song by ear. It is not up to you to take care of how things are. Very few people can stand it. Some may turn back, and the mind is eagerly waiting to welcome your return. But in satsang you are encouraged to endure this squeeze and the discomfort. It is only for a limited time like this, only for as long the Beingness needs to burp up some old, trapped energies. Some inner spring-cleaning is going on. It is a good sign.

If you wish to drink pure water,
then go to the Source.

THE SEED 'I AM'

In the crystal ball of Consciousness is contained the sense of the Seer perceiving, reporting and engaging with the experience of diversity, outside and within the form through which it is also expressing. The sense 'I Am' is the seed out of which all of this is sprouting, and which is perceived by that 'I Am' intuition. The 'I Am' cannot express itself without the form. Without the form It cannot experience.

The Seer of 'I Am', no one can see. You cannot use your intellect beyond the 'I Am'. So, what is it that knows even the intellect itself? Don't use your imagination, imagination is watched! Who is still thinking? Even your tendency towards thinking, along with the thinking itself, is watched from That which is beyond thought. So, what is the use of thought? It is redundant.

Many of you fear to question beyond the intellectual capacity of the mind. There is an idea that 'no mind' equals craziness, 'If I lose my mind I am going to be mad!' Find out what is holding onto mind or giving up mind. Because all of this is mind! You are That in which mind with all its notions and ideas, even madness, are contained. How can you, in discovering who you are, become crazy?

There is nothing wrong with thought. There is nothing wrong with any object. Just some mistaken identification creates this mischief and you are here to discover this self-deception. In examining the 'I', you will find out that 'I' belongs to nobody.

'I Am' is Freedom, 'I Am' is Being. 'I Am' is un-mixable, pure; without 'I Am' nothing exists. It is the unfading perfume of the Divine shining in each body. That Divinity in my body is talking to that same Divinity in your body. The One looking through my eyes is the same One looking through your eyes. You are to discover this Truth, it will reveal itself. And you who discover It, and to whom It is revealed, are It itself.

There is no need to scratch your head about it. It reveals itself to itself, not to another.

SUBTLER THAN SPACE

When it comes to the point of self-enquiry, it doesn't work for me because it feels very mental. Instead, I shift the focus of my attention on space rather than on the objects that appear in space.

Wonderful! Before, you were itemising what was coming up which creates a sort of claustrophobia in the Beingness. Now, you focus on the space within which this play appears, so your vision is all-inclusive, panoramic. When seeing and space become one, obviously the world becomes quiet.
   Does your quality of life deteriorate or flourish?

I am very happy.

Already there is a natural sense of joy, and a relaxation in your Beingness. Whatever appears in space, disappears in space, and yet the space is not waiting for it to go. Even if some manifestation is filling up space, space is not troubled. In time it will pass. This far you've come, very good!
   Now, one more step. In the statement, 'I focus on space rather than the object' there is a sense of choice: 'I can go with

the object or I can go with space. If I go with the object: turbulence comes! When I go with space: stillness is present. I like the stillness; I think I will stay with the stillness.' What is the constitution of the one focusing on and choosing space?

It knows that it is still watching space.

Then it must be subtler, because it can even watch space.

Sometimes there is the sense I am that within which this exercise is happening – just for an instant – and then it shifts again to some sort of doer focusing.

Awareness can never be an object. It cannot be perceived phenomenally. Being consciously conscious of Awareness, is an action you cannot do! Something is simply occurring. What you are searching for has already happened, actually it didn't happen; it is before all happening. It is already so, but there is some movement that says, 'I still don't get it' being believed in. You will come to see that the 'I' that needed to 'get it' was itself the apparent obstacle because it created some dichotomy.

I am using concepts in order to remove your concepts. And when they are removed – my concepts and your concepts – then what will remain is already here, now! Closer than contact! Closer than intimacy! You are searching with the mind, and mind can only search for an object. Can mind find the subject, in which mind itself appears as an object?

If you don't get it, it is okay. It doesn't have to make sense. Only this needs to be recognised: You are looking for something, but you are already looking from there. Stay with this recognition. You have come to a beautiful place where you are not picking up or salvaging anything. You've seen clearly: What appears on the screen also belongs to the screen. It comes and goes. Sometimes there is space, silence, stillness. This is the joy of non-identification. Let the objects appear, you are neither holding nor pushing them, they simply appear by themselves according to their own laws.

When you are not identifying with objects, immediately there is a natural sense of joy and peace. Then Love will respond, "Now you are no longer preoccupied with 'other', you are available for me. I will come."

I am the Great Waters.
Upon My face, the primordial pen of Mahamaya
writes incessantly
the lives and destinies of all living beings.
Every wave, each ripple,
the subtlest movement — is My dancing.
Yet I — the pure Reality,
remain ever untouched, unaffected.
Glorious and beyond all concepts,
I — the Unimaginable,
the Formless Absolute,
Alone AM.

AN APPOINTMENT WITH
THE BUDDHA

Nothing is happening to you. This is just your game, your play. There is nothing to write home about; there is nothing going on that would even fill a postcard!

How can you be afraid of your Shiva Being, who is empty of all intention, empty of time, empty of cause and effect, empty of tomorrow, empty of life and death? All has been emptied out. See, it's just a dream arising in This and the dream is part of This! The dream is part of Its play, of Its magnificence! And you will have removed your noise. Then what remains is motionless, immutable and pure – indivisible Existence. Nataraj!

The body is afraid of all that!

The body is not afraid of This, the body is longing for This! Longing for the mind to relax into This.

The mind is afraid then.

But where is the mind? Mind itself is a thought! Seeing is taking place, and the seeing becomes empty. All the senses are functioning but they become silent. And what is behind all of these? The Infinite! The Infinite is behind, in front, above, underneath and beyond all of that!

There is an insidious virus of disbelief, and this virus is sucking the attention. But that too is seen. It is seen as the voice that's been nearest, this phantom 'I'.

It is like a holding on . . .

Don't identify with anything that is holding on. 'Holding on' is nothing but a thought – a thought holding onto a thought.

These are all just ideas! This is not you! Why are you hiding from the fullness of what you are? Why are you afraid? It is not you! When you talk like this, I don't accept it, I don't believe you! And I have no interest in what you speak! Each time I meet you, you are the Lord Himself. But you're posing as the Lord in denial of Himself – is it possible?

You keep putting things in front of yourself, 'This stops me!' Nonsense! Nothing stops you! Who told you so? You as 'you' don't exist except as a thought. You are only worth meeting when you are not.

[*Silence*]

I have an appointment to meet the Buddha in Tiruvannamalai. And I am waiting.

BEING HONEY

When this direct experience comes, something feels it needs more.

Inspect this need for more! See if it is anything other than a thought invitation. The ideas we have of awakening keep us in constant limbo. We keep waiting for something to happen. It is as if we carry a checklist of awakening around with us, convinced that our images and notions of the Truth are correct. A shortlist of our favourite ideas about awakening to Truth reads something like this: 'All my problems will finally go once I'm awake', 'I will not feel pain anymore when I know who I am', 'Freedom means I will be in constant bliss'. From this we conclude that if problems appear in life, we can't be there. If the capacity to feel pain is still present, we can't possibly know who we are, and for as long as bliss is not showing up, we are most definitely not free. These fantasies trap us in a continual spiral of separation. In fact, this checklist of what should be there if one is free undermines one's very Freedom.

There are many thoughts like these swirling through the seeker's mind! But thought by itself has no power. It is only your belief in a thought that gives it life. Consequently, you think these obstacles into existence. They then become your experience, and in turn thicken the illusion which the mind then battles with as if it was never self-imposed. Something seems to be habitual at perpetuating and sustaining the sense of an independent self.

I can see I don't need the thought, but still it is there.

So, let the thought be there! Don't even try to push it away. Ignore it! This is what the sages have done. They gradually ignored the suggestions of thought out of existence. By not giving these conditioned and repetitive thoughts any attention, there is clarity when a pure thought issues from Emptiness. No angst or need is associated with it. Pure thought is weightless in that it has no hidden agenda; it is alive and flows into action spontaneously. And no training is required to discern between the two. Your only task is: When the thoughts appear that say, 'Come with us', you exercise the power to recognise that you are just the watching. The invitation then loses its appeal and natural discernment arises from the stillness that remains.

Is it really this simple? Yes, it really is this simple. This is why your mind rejects it with this decree, 'It is not enough!'

Down through the ages, the wise ones, in their own unique ways, have revealed this perpetual cause of human suffering: You want to taste honey; you don't want to be honey.

Honey cannot taste honey! It is impossible. Because you want to continue tasting, the path to the Truth is never ending. That's why you are so attracted to 'Seven Steps to Freedom'. And after the seventh step, you keep introducing even more;

all the books, and the various spiritual paths and practices come to serve you. You use them to postpone this discovery of your Self, which is immediate. All the different flavours are where your interest lies and so the Truth eludes you. You say you want Freedom but you want freedom in instalments. Freedom Is. It cannot be separated into neat packages, or steps.

You ask, "What is the purpose of being free if there is no taste?" All the beings are addicted to the taste of experiencing: the contrast, the friction, the tension, the unpredictability, the drama, the promise. Even the failure, you love.

The sages enjoy more purely; without attachment, without addiction, without craving, without need, without comparison. Their enjoyment is fresh, the same way you used to enjoy as a very young child. Sages enjoy the world, but they do not suffer it. An experience is just a flavour washing through the body of Joy that they are. There is no self invested in the experience. So there is nothing to be gained by it and nothing to be lost. There is a bliss that is beyond the tasting of honey. Being Honey, that is the highest!

That which says:
'My mind is too strong',
is the mind itself.

An illusion,
strengthened by belief.

WHEN PAIN AND PEACE
ARE ONE

*I want to go back to this experience 'I am That'. There was only peace
and now I feel so much tension!*

Tension only means tension is present, nothing more. What
labels are you fastening to tension that make it such a significant
and unpleasant phenomenon? It does not have to disturb you.
It is quite possible to be very tense and simultaneously, be one
hundred percent at peace.

*But there was so much pain this morning during meditation that I
couldn't focus on the question 'Who am I?'*

Maybe this question was not what was required at the time.
Sometimes it is a matter of just allowing whatever is happening;
without judgement, without pushing away, without holding
on and making it into an event. You feel pain, so what?

I would like to stop it and feel fine!

This wanting it to stop is what is causing the trouble! Let the pain be there, watch it! This is real enquiry. When pain, be it emotional or physical in expression, is magnified to the utmost intensity, then you stand the greatest chance to see what you are not! This doesn't mean you choose to martyr yourself or neglect the body's health. If a doctor needs to be called, fine, you do what you have to do but at the same time make full use of the opportunity to look and see. And if there is nothing to be done, surrendering into the pain is essential. Fighting it only exaggerates the discomfort. It is clear to me that you are giving some interpretation to this experience that makes it noisier, more miserable and disagreeable.

Due to the sacred energy of this holy mountain, Arunachula, or the fire of satsang, some physical and emotional reactions occur with increased virility. Bodily ailments are more uncomfortable and debilitating, whilst emotions are louder. This exaggeration makes it hard for the mind to distract from the 'dis-ease' it feels. It is forced to face what it would prefer to suppress, or run away from. You are being given the perfect, tailor-made opportunity to remain quiet and observe that these symptoms, like all phenomena, will pass. What Grace!

Let the reactions happen. Hand over your existence to Existence. I say to you, come Home. All you are afraid of losing is keeping you in this pain.

It is said that fish cannot live in water that is too clean.
Similarly, thoughts cannot thrive
when the attention is immersed in the Self.

CAVIAR OF THE BEINGNESS

Your remark earlier about the birth pangs that come when we are born into Emptiness, which sounded like needing to go through hell to get to heaven, really irritated me. I wonder how many years it will take?

When you start living by your own experience, by your own Self-dependency, these are great years. For so long you've been cultivating a way that seemed to work in the world, but it wasn't enough. Something was left hungering for lasting satisfaction. If it wasn't like that, would you have come here? Despite any resistance and fears of your mind, you found your way here. You can trust that this Power which brought you here is now satisfying itself. It's removing this dreaming mind. Of course, irritation will come up, because you cannot rely on your own power anymore. Everything you used to count on is leaving you. Your boundaries, your safety holds, your walking sticks and your life support system, everything has been taken away from you. Something, deeply upset about this, is screaming, 'I want freedom but not if it is painful and brings discomfort!' You want it in pill form so you get it all done today!

The fear of the loss of identity, the fear of the loss of control, the fear of abandonment, the fear of giving up your dreams, the fear of the loss of your attachments come up like serpents to frighten you. They derive power through your attention. You support them because they have meaning for you. Thus energised, they start molesting your peace.

That Which Is, is not difficult to find – no, It is here even now! It is just that the discovery of this Truth seems to threaten your worldly attachments. You don't realise that everything you are afraid to let go of is nothing! It only figures big in your mind! The apparent gap between yourself and Reality is only the distance of a concept.

If it is hurting too much to let go then don't, instead try something softer: Take a look at why you are holding on. If even this is too hard for you, find out who is giving up and who is holding on?

Even this you don't want to do? Do you feel threatened even by this question?

Only that which is effortless can be called natural. What you love is effortlessness. Effort is needed to pursue everything other than What Is. You cannot pursue What Is because you already are What Is.

Perhaps your hesitation is rooted in ideas about what Self-discovery will bring you. If you've heard that freedom is the same as emptiness, you may be asking yourself what is free about that? Nothing is going on in emptiness. It is not very appealing to your mind, because for the mind it means death. But we are not inviting you to enter the mind's version of emptiness. We are leading you into direct experience of dynamic Emptiness, your very own Self. The instant you discover This, you won't ever deny It again, because you are getting into your primal Being, your primal Joy; at long last, the thirst for lasting satisfaction is also quenched.

On which side of awakening are you listening? I am speaking directly to that Which Is. I am speaking from That to That itself.

It doesn't need to go on a pilgrimage to meet itself. It doesn't need to do any spiritual gymnastics to be itself. Why should it be frustrating? For whom is it frustrating? You should find out! 'You' cannot be frustrated! You are aware of frustration arising as some energy. That within which the frustration energy is perceived isn't and can't ever be frustrated! I am showing you the caviar of the Beingness, but you are turning it into cat food!

[*Laughter followed by long silence*]

Hold on only to the simple feeling of existence — 'I Am' —
that sweet and Formless intuition within.
Keep quiet until the one who keeps . . . disappears.

THE ORIGINAL BEING

I am a teacher, but the structures in schools are academic-mind based and I have dropped into a place deeper than that. My dilemma is whether to stay or to honour what is going on inwardly, or is there somewhere in between?

The answer for me is very clear. You must go deeply with the calling of your own Heart and you must do it completely, so you are not trying to swim and walk on the beach at the same time. It is not possible. Sometimes, the dilemma deepens more when there is a feeling that one should not turn away from the challenge, 'Surely there is some way I can bring more heart-quality into this space.' But this is not necessarily what is wanted of you.

Let go as much as the calling allows you, into a deeper place of understanding and insight. Really surrender to that Power, which has already set in motion the calling and the pull towards itself. Our own human limitations of perception can never really fathom Its wisdom.

This Power is not different from your Self. Whatever it does, you will come to see that it is in perfect harmony. The more you imbibe this and come Home, even without effort or intention, others will somehow benefit from your existence, and in ways that maybe you are not even aware of! This is the power of Silence. In the presence of those who dwell in their original Being – who are free from limited thinking and limited identification – such effect, such influence, such beauty takes place.

You are no other than the original Being. You came to find this out, don't let anything delay you. There is nothing more worthy of discovery in this form than to know who you are. You are not betraying your profession, and every support will be given to you.

Trust, that life holds you when you make a step like this. It is not merely theory – it is possible to wake up, to be entirely free of suffering, free of doubt and free of fear. In turn, you bring peace to the people that try to hinder you from your journey in the first place.

What can stand in the way when your search is for total liberation from your own conditioning? Align yourself with Truth and life aligns itself with you. Grace is your benevolent and constant ally.

Life is not so unkind
as to allow
all your dreams to be fulfilled.

HIDING IN THE PILLOW
OF GOD

I want to get there.

Please examine this 'I want to get there'. At first glance it
seems a very auspicious thought, but accompanying it, unseen
on the other side of the coin, is its silent counterpart, 'I am
not there, I am separate'. The two sides co-exist, feeding your
mind-bank of conceptual separation. So, don't touch either
side of the coin. Don't touch this coin at all. Throw it away.
What remains?

And the answer I don't want! It is the question that has
significance. It is a perfect mirror. Let the question unfold
and reflect within your being. Don't think about it! We are so
good at picking up further coins with 'I' stamped on them, in
the effort to get somewhere, or to get something. Do not
enter any movement at all, however subtle. Where do you
need to go? The Truth has always been here. More immediate
than any thought, more intimate than your very breath.

Any feeling arising out of this introspection, do not identify
with it. All emotions, like thoughts, are tourists not tenants.
Exist through your eyes alone. Again I ask you, what remains?

If it isn't already here, drop it! Waiting isn't appropriate. Neither is expectation; that which is expecting is also mind. That which watches mind's expectation is beyond expectation. Nothing can get in between you and It. Nothing can obscure It.

There is peace and stillness now.

I don't believe you! Your energy does not convey this. You are That within which peace and stillness arise. Peace and stillness are the perfume of that perfume-less Flower that you are. Don't create, don't imagine.

I really don't know what to do.

Even there, in the bedroom of the Divine itself, still this 'I' is there. Hiding in the pillow of God!

I want to escape.

Let this 'I' who wants to escape, escape and you stay! Why tie yourself to this serpent who has been whispering inside your head for all these years? Identify this one that says, 'I want to escape'. Is it you?

I want to stay.

That voice also is not yours, for so long as it is felt as yours you will feel you have to leave. It is just another 'I want' coin to be tossed aside. Leave these judgements alone, and identify,

'This voice is not my voice. Something inside me wants to go, but I am staying.' As what are you staying? And is there any effort in this remaining? A person cannot remain, only what remains, remains. And you are That.

Give up the idea of a journey to Truth and Truth is instantly revealed. Give up this idea that you are near. This concept will take you to another birth, another opportunity. It is itself avoidance. And this silly, 'I still don't get it', don't pay any attention to this serpent's voice.

Keep quiet; let's see if you are fit just to remain quiet. Your malignant relationship with mind as master is over. The mind can be used for normal service but can never help you to be who you are.

No heady philosophy is required to know your Self, just this mirroring. Do you have the courage to look into this, your own mirror? There was a time when you were not ready to see. Now, something brings you here; take a look.

Take a look or leave.

If you do what is right from your Heart,
it cannot turn out to be wrong for someone else.

REMOVING THE CATARACT OF 'I'

No question is left.

When no questions are left, peace remains.

Yes, there is peace, but I can't describe it.

No one can describe this peace! No one has been able to convey This with words because It is before words, you see? If you touch your mind, the mind will decorate further this raw material of manifestation. It will add ego-filled interpretation, such as sentiment, desire and resistance. These distortions are layered upon your original seeing. Always based on the 'I', these interpretations create the world of duality, of 'other', and then fear and incompleteness are welcomed into becoming a seeming reality.

When free of the need to judge or identify, no energy leaks out of the senses; they become quiet. Only pure perceiving remains. When this State is present, you don't sleep very much but you are never tired. You don't want anything; and when you don't want anything you are free! No expectation, no anticipation, nothing to reject. Natural silence, natural peace are present. I am speaking to that very State within which the mind wants to do something about it: 'What more do I need to do?', 'Should I meditate more?' You are That already! You cannot improve It! It is only awaiting recognition. And, what is going to recognise it even? The recognition itself is arising out of It. So effortlessly, without giving up the questions, the questions slip away from you.

Your intuitive sense of Self arises out of Nothing.

It just is, arising of itself. It is happiness and sadness.

And yet, it is beyond them also. It plays through them in manifestation. Even this Silence is beyond silence, you see? It is your Self. It is your Abode, but nothing, no 'thing', abides there. It is referred to as your Buddha-Nature, but no Buddha is there. I am 'you' and I am 'I', and I am even beyond these.

We've been peeling away in order to find That which cannot be recognised phenomenally and is spontaneously experienced without words, because it is wordless Space. This forest of conceptual identification, has eclipsed the intuitive recognition which is both silent and Silence itself. We are meant to go through this forest and then somehow come out the other side. Now and again, a Christ walks out, a Buddha walks out. Sometimes one of us stumbles out and goes back in again. But some come out, and coming out of it means realising I am not the one who's been struggling amongst the trees. I am not the forest dweller. I dreamed it somehow and yet it is also connected with me. It is not the definition of what I am, but somehow it is the expression arising out of my Self. It is now known that it is not the Absolute, it is just a play believed in.

WHEREVER I AM, I AM STILL

I do not have a standard answer for questions. There is no standard answer. It is not just about answering the question, but also answering the questioner, and that makes the big difference.

You can believe in God, but you can't 'believe' in the Self; you can only 'be' the Self. Your Beingness is totally silent. It is not bothered about concepts and problems. Only the mind is concerned, not the Heart. If you stay in the realm of the mind, you will never land in the realm of your own Being completely.

This is the main discovery: Wherever I go, I am never outside of the Self.

Nothing I can do, or not do, can affect that Awareness-Self. Which I am.

Every person offers
a little reflection
  of the One Self
But a sage is like a huge mirror
in whose Compassionate presence
the disharmonious is seen.

Many avoid this mirroring
but those who continue to look

Come to see ...

The face of God.

BEING THE ONE
WITHOUT HISTORY

Last time I came in front of you to ask a question, my heart started beating so much that I don't dare ask another one today. I just wanted to come here again, just to sit for two or three minutes.

Why not stay eternally?

I want to stay here eternally, but it depends very much on you.

No, it does not depend on me. That does not depend on me. You cannot stay on this physical plane eternally. Why do you want to stay anywhere for any amount of time? Why not stay someplace eternal? Even to say 'to stay' is not true. You cannot stay anywhere that is eternal. You only must get rid of 'you'. Then what's eternal will manifest. Where there's a 'you' there's time and trouble.

    This personal 'I', the 'me', is like a broken finger, everywhere it goes it causes trouble, everything it touches it feels pain. The one identified with 'I' thinks that anything that happens in his life is caused by his environment including the people around him. He will say, 'Others cause me pain', 'My life's circumstances are responsible'. It's endless. Very few take the opportunity, or are interested in, finding out the source of their troubles, their suffering.

I tell you, it is 'I'. 'I' is the cause of your troubles. It is because you have made your nest inside the sense of a personal 'I' that you are bound to suffer. Don't fix your life. Find this 'I' and see what happens. How long can your troubles last?

When you say 'I' want to be here for three minutes, three minutes most certainly will come to an end, and what will 'I' have gained?

You, as I know you, are eternal, and I love the company of That. Speak as Consciousness. Speak to me as Consciousness and not as a person. Over six billion human beings speak on the basis that they are a person. Their conversations are rooted in the idea that 'I'm a person and you are a person', 'This is my life', 'This is what I've accomplished', 'I show you my life; you show me yours'. Who wants to know? Whose life is so interesting? Speak as Consciousness! Fresh! Do not speak from the past! What good is the past? Nobody wants it. No one eats yesterday's food. Nobody reads yesterday's newspaper. Why should you talk of past? Don't speak about future either! There's something that is so fresh that there cannot be any history of Now. Be the One who has no history!

I see nobody who is bound. I keep asking you where are you bound? Why do you say, "I am bound?" Why do you say, "I want to be free?" I understand this plea and feel deeply touched. Let's check and see if we can determine what the problem really is. What we'll uncover is a conviction that all is not well. And when we check this out to find out why, we'll discover that you are identifying with death. You are identifying with something that doesn't endure, that has no longevity. You've fallen in love with time. You've fallen in love with objects, with ideas in service to what is transient. This is how trouble comes. This is how confusion has entered your Being.

The life force
flows effortlessly.

Effort appears with the idea
that there is a 'someone'
having an action to perform.

LINGO OF ONENESS

Since last night I feel in my heart that I'm united with all people. I feel like a little pin on the board in service of existence. This sensation is full of emotion and commotion. Trembling and trepidation is there. It's like I have to let it go, because in this sensation I feel there is some danger for my ego.

I have heard people say this before: "I had this experience and now we are all one together." And I want to ask, we're one as what? In what way are 'we' one? We're still keeping our 'we'-ness. What is this 'we' that is one, and one with what? This is what I want to know. I want to find out if you've just learnt the lingo of Oneness but in truth an idea that 'we' plus 'we' equals one persists for you still.

Don't dismiss this experience. It's fine. Something is revealing through this a greater truth. Perhaps your deeper intention to come forward is to clarify an interpretation that's coming for you that as yet is incomplete.

The feeling of Oneness does not go around collecting all the beings to bring them into the 'Club of Oneness'. The sense of Oneness is the sense of the Unicity of Being. Oneness does not refer to a feeling that I am the same as all beings. No, not at all. It is rather that the sense that I as an individual entity cannot be found. And in place of this finding of my non-existence there is an intuitive sense that there is just This! This! The entire spectrum of the experiential world is what I am and even beyond that!

Let me repeat this! It is not that there's an 'I' that is one with all the other 'I's in the world. No, it's that the 'I' as a psychological entity, which carries a feeling of independent doership, is not found, and in its place a sense of Unity appears. What's realised is that only the Self is here. Only the pure Self is here. There are not two chairs in your heart, a big chair for the big Self and a little chair for the little self. There's just the Self, you see? It's from here that a sense of 'other' forms. All are forms of the one Self.

Once this Union with the Self has become your own reality, what you used to perceive as another person will have blurred to nothing more than a unique fragrance of the Self. You will perceive the same Self in all beings. There is a saying, 'I am not seeing the world as it is, I am seeing the world as I am.' In other words, when you are the Self then the 'other' is also the Self, because the Self does not see 'other'.

Superficially we can continue speaking the language of separation and appearances. The body is seen and felt and a certain amount of conditioning and education will still persist in the play of existence we call our life. You will still recognise your children; outwardly, you may still have the same career. The Consciousness continues playing like this, but all of it arises within a deeper seeing and understanding that these are just appearances in me. The body also is known as an appearance inside the Self that I am. This is not a teaching. There will be a deep intuitive certainty about this for you because the feeling 'I am the body' is replaced simply with the intuition 'I Am'. Mysteriously, in this knowing, the effortless conviction that I am eternal and what is here is eternal naturally arises.

From this perspective, everything becomes this spontaneous Existence. There isn't any room left for any ideas like you being a servant of God – a notion that seems humble enough, but there's also a 'servant of God' ego. God is not helpless that He needs the assistance of human beings. He doesn't cry out, "Help! Help! Help me to do this thing, please!" [*Laughter*]

So, be quiet and realise the Truth of your Oneness.

Freedom is free but not cheap.
In fact, it is priceless.
It will cost you
your world, your attachments,
your life — your own self.
You will be paying this over and over
until you are drained of all 'you' have
and all 'you' have saved up.
You will exchange all this
for that which 'you' cannot have
— your eternal Being.

GIVING UP THE FIRM

Who is behind this whole manifestation? Look, and you will discover that it is going on by itself! When you see this, then your consciousness becomes unoccupied. Until then, it is being occupied by the doer sense, 'I must do something, I must understand'.

Effort is required to become, but what effort is required to be? So, remain as what remains; witness spontaneous Existence. It is not chaotic. Whatever goes on, goes on, and it does rather well. The supposed manager – mind – is causing a lot of trouble. And no, we are not just firing the manager, we are giving up the firm!

See if the universe stops.

Many of you are not enjoying the cream of life, because you've purchased the mind's version of how things should be. This idea has cut you off from the Source of yourself, so you no longer flow. Disharmony results, and suffering. You are the Self, the Absolute, expressing as the spontaneous, but you don't know it. You don't even trust it! You think, 'What will happen if I give up my control? My world will fall apart!' So you remain in ignorance to the excellence of the Beingness that you are.

Existence is looking after the body. Stay as the 'I Am' – the intuitive sense that nobody gave you; that is and has always been present. Out of 'I Am' everything is manifesting. It merely observes the mechanism of the universe which is moved by this vital force, this breath in your body, the animating power in all bodies. It is a mystery, and it cannot be solved. So don't try! Observe.

Who you really are is not predictable. Mind is predictable in its attempts to control the spontaneous. Fearing the unknown, the mind simultaneously arises out of the Unknown, which provides the space for the mind to play as the unknown and the apparent known. This play is not your business.

Don't worry about anything. Be like a child in the lap of God. Just enjoy. Neither the policing of thoughts, nor manning an immigration office for feelings is required. You can relax. Yes. Relax.

The Infinite seems so unending;
surely, I'll be lost in it.

You can only be lost if you are a form.
Forms are seen in you — the Formless.
If you are the Formless itself,
where exactly could you be lost
when you have no boundaries?

THE 'I' IS CALLED
INTO THE WITNESS BOX

Bhagavan says that the 'I Am' is the Reality. Holding the 'I Am' with effort he calls 'vichara' or self-enquiry. When this becomes effortless it is Self-realisation. In my understanding and experience the 'I Am'-ness is not phenomenal. It has no special taste and no qualities.

Then why are you referring to it as 'it'? Who is talking about 'it'? When you speak about 'I Am', what are you observing? Sri Ramana at another time distinguishes between the 'gross body' and the 'subtle body'. The 'I Am' is the 'subtle body'. How can you say that 'I Am' isn't phenomenal or without quality? How could you know 'I Am' if it was quality-less or non-phenomenal? Are you speaking from your own experience? You are assuming here.

For sure this is an interpretation of the mind when it is outside the 'I Am'. When the attention is inside the 'I Am' there isn't a 'me' and 'I Am'.

Even when there's a 'me' inside the 'I Am' as you have put it, the awareness of that intuition 'I Am' is still present. It hasn't gone anywhere, has it? There is awareness of the sense of existence. 'I am' means 'I exist'. You are not claiming not to exist now that a sense of a 'me' is present, are you? What would make such a claim anyway?

The 'I Am' must be there before any knowing and perception can be. All knowledge and all experiences are the functioning that is sourced in and arises out of this intuition 'I Am'.

So, what enjoys deep sleep? Is it the 'I Am'?

No, it is not the 'I Am', because you are unconscious in deep sleep. Neither body nor mind – which we mistakenly regard as the centre of gravity of being and knowingness – exist for you in that state. Still something is capable to impart knowledge of deep sleep when Consciousness, body and mind reappear. So it must be a much, much subtler Knowingness that remains. Deep sleep is enjoyed in the presence of some power we simply refer to as Awareness. Awareness is the constant in the absence and presence of all experiences and is present even now in the waking state and is prior to 'I Am'. It's from Awareness that the 'I Am' is watched.

So when you say, 'observe the observer', the way I hear this is that you are directing the 'I Am' to observe the ego observer.

No, forget about these things! What you know is that observing takes place. You have a sense of 'I am observing' and of 'I am observing objects'. Question who or what is this 'I' that observes? No one asks this question.

Don't become mental about this. Just allow this pointer to happen inwardly and see. Something moves as a result of this question. Can the observing centre – the core of observing – also be observed?

Forget who is going to carry out this instruction. Simply follow this advice.

In your experience, are you that which is aware of even the 'I Am'?

Of course! And so are you! Don't separate me. We are one in This. And my question to you is, can't you see that even the most subtle, intuitive sense of yourself – we call it simply the intuition 'I Am' – itself is observed?

Once someone asked me, "Mooji, are you always in touch with your intuition?" I said, "No! Who's going to be in touch with intuition?" It's just that intuition is here. Who is doing it? Nobody's doing it.

This is the mistake: You experience a 'me' and you know of the 'I Am'. You think that it's the responsibility of the 'me' feeling to do something to unite with the sense of 'I Am' and to stay there once that is achieved. This 'me', this 'I', is always shape-shifting. No one can catch it. As soon as you look for it, it slips under the carpet. You look and it's gone, you cannot find it. Why? Find out why!

Only the one who's fixed on this enquiry and remains quiet will come to some certitude about this sense 'I'. The one that is the doership sense of 'I', the 'I' that moves, the 'I' that carries out the work, the 'I' that arises as a seeker trying to get somewhere; has anybody caught this 'I' apart from thought, memory, belief? Has it been found? This 'I' has been making all the noise in the world. Now it's being called into the witness box itself. We demand: Present yourself! How would it show up? This is introspection. This is enquiry. The power is with you to find out.

All that is perceivable, all that is knowable, must appear in front of you. You're the one who comments about it, so you must be earlier. In order for observing to take place there must be some distance. This is what 'observing' means. 'Observing' implies that there must be at least two: The observer and the observed along with the functioning of observing. Who is this 'I', the observer? Who will embrace this question? Allow this examination some room! If this kind of investigation is coming alive in you, then you are already in Grace, already Grace is there with you. You won't need many more questions now. I can count them, two or three at the very most remain to be asked if you've come to this point of looking.

*The apparent distance
between yourself and the Beloved,
is only the distance of a thought.*

*But that thought believed in,
brings suffering to the world.*

TAKE A LOOK AT THE OBSERVER

Remain as the Self! Stay with the habit of identifying with the Self as much as you can. Gradually, the volume and intensity of thought activity will fall away and only the Self will remain.

Is there no other way apart from what you are suggesting? I find continuous identification with the Self tiresome, if not impossible.

It is tiring because you are trying so hard with the mind. Another way is to ignore each thought as it appears. Because you are so accustomed to giving attention to thoughts, it is likely that sooner or later you will become involved with them again. Although similar in effect, you may find the advice to stay as the Self easier than ignoring thoughts, as it is a passive rather than an active focus. As the habit of remaining as the Self strengthens, ignoring thoughts will become easier.

Your advice is to observe the observer, but each time I try to do this I become very mental and soon I am left with a headache. Where am I going wrong?

At first, most people think that observing the mind means simply paying attention to the various activities appearing in the mind. This is the way it can be interpreted. But the advice is to remain detached in the state of witnessing without becoming involved with the movements of the mind.

Don't merely watch the activity; instead observe the inner reaction to the activity. This is more intimate than just watching the mind-play. These reactions show how much personal involvement has been cultivated; where there is identification and 'noise'. When I say 'noise' I speak of the inner turbulence — resistance and excitement — which disturbs your peace. As soon as these tendencies are recognised, the next step is to ask, who, what and where is the one who is identified? Can a face be put to it? Is there an actual, tangible entity in residence as 'I'? Find out! To answer these questions, the attention must be introverted — fixed on the source of the arising activity.

There is nothing there. When searched for, nothing is found in such a position.

Good. What is making this discovery?

My mind. My Consciousness.

No, you are speculating. Your Heart is not present in this answer.

This is where I get stuck.

This is not true. 'Getting stuck' or an apparent block is only another thought. Don't accept this thought so readily. For the moment, don't identify with any thought; remain apart – unassociated. Then find out as what do you stand apart? Go into this with full attention and an open heart. Feel your way.

But this is also observed, isn't it?

You move too quickly and jump to conclusions. When attention is fixed on its Source, division cannot remain, and any sense of separation gets merged in the Source.

I am saying this merging is watched also, is it not?

How can it be, if the watcher gets merged? What remains is only the unified field of Being. There is no question or questioner left. The restlessness arising from the pain and noise of separation ceases.

I would just like you to clarify this point: Can the observer be observed?

There is a mental smell about your questioning. With this approach, nothing will come of this quest of yours. You will be merely fencing with questions. 'Cleverness' of this kind is the mind's ploy to avoid you diving into the real discovery that awaits beyond the mind's capacity to understand.

I am deeply keen to find lasting peace and inner satisfaction.

Then are you sufficiently clear on the other points so far discussed that you are ready to move on to a new one? If you are truly keen, a mere mental answer to the question, 'Can the observer be observed?' will not satisfy you. You must find out the real answer for yourself, by enquiring wholeheartedly into the identity of that which arises as 'I' within you. Properly pursued, this question does not merely produce a conceptual response; it devours the questioner, and only the serenity and peace of the Self remains.

UNTOUCHABLE

The natural state of mind is to be silent, empty, open. It exists without intention! If you think you need to practise silence, find silence, keep silence, then you have misunderstood. All this, the whole universe, is happening in Silence!

It is not about running to find some silence. It is to recognise the Silence which cannot be disturbed wherever you find yourself, whatever the circumstances, however loud the noise. Reactions of any nature do not exist. It is not a behaviour or an enforcement – you and the Silence are the same.

All this talking, this pointing, is only to reveal your own Silence. And it doesn't take time! When you stand in front of the mirror, it doesn't say, 'Look, I am busy right now, come back in half an hour!' So powerful is the mirror of enquiry, immediately you are seen! And then you know the Indescribable, the Formless directly. Maybe you cannot speak about it, but your suffering is over. Your fears are over. You conquer death itself!

So many of you, at the nearest opportunity of discovery, make excuses and run away, afraid to burn the last attachment to 'I'. The opportunity is to face it, to feel it and to see that you are the Untouchable.

Feeling stuck is simply a thought believed in.
Remove the belief, and stuckness vanishes.

If a room has been kept in darkness for a thousand years,
when the window opens —
does it take a thousand years for the darkness to leave?

Likewise, in an instant,
the light of Truth expels the darkness of ignorance.

AMNESIA IN THE BEINGNESS

I come with a lot of resistance. There is great fear that I will lose myself. I really want to be on the path but then I don't follow through.

You have to decide who you are. Misidentification is what is holding you in a vice. If you are the Self, there will be no more fear. If you are the egoic mind, then there is all-consuming fear that everything you 'are' is going to be sucked into emptiness.

There is fear that life will not be so entertaining if I become silent.

When life is so entirely fascinating and entertaining, you will not have the attraction for satsang, so I don't completely believe you. Something is looking within also.

Yes, it is.

And when you look within, what happens?

Well, there is peace and joy.

These are but mere trifles . . . [*laughter*] and what else?

Then it is as if I hit a wall.

A wall? There cannot be a wall. When perceived through the mind it can seem there is a wall and that you have to break this wall to go beyond, but these are just ideas because it is impossible for the Self to be apart from you, except as a projection.

You are the Self in which the idea of coming towards the Self is appearing. But who will accept this statement? Because apparently the evidence shows: that you are coming into dissolution. Arunachala is one of the few places where questioning of this assumption is being encouraged! Yes, dissolution is happening, but not of your Self. You are identifying with the ego's experience and that is why this wall appears real for you. This wall is the ego itself. In response to its fear of the loss of autonomy and the loss of pleasure, it is trying to defend its existence with the idea that all the Buddhas are boring!

Right, they just sit in caves. [Laughter]

So why bother coming to satsang then? [*Laughs*]

I don't know. I just keep coming back.

Yes, you keep coming back because something inside you knows there is nothing really to be found in the outer world. And when you are here there is joy, there is peace. Nobody is troubled by joy or peace. What you're being troubled by is the feeling that while you're in joy and peace you're missing the party elsewhere, isn't it?

Yes.

And this is restlessness. Forget about going to the Self or away from the Self. You are the Self! Give up these ideas: 'If I go towards peace then I lose so much' and 'If I go towards the world there is so much pleasure, so much joy'. Whichever way your mind turns or your body acts, it is possible to remain as the Self. You are the Witness of both attraction to worldly pleasure and seeking of serenity. This Witness you are right now and have always been. For as long as you are not clear about this, it will appear to you as if your choice will result in a consequence, which will either be good or bad. And then there is angst, 'Do I take the blue pill or the red pill?'

You don't have to take any pill. Just recognise, 'I am here as Existence.' Don't attach any ideas to Existence. Don't give any image to It. Remain in this image-less, unassociated Presence. Does that sound so painful?

That sounds good.

Stay as you are. Where did this idea to go here or to go there come from? From the mind. You don't need to go anywhere. Remain.

In recognising this, enormous stillness is present. You won't find any separation between what you are and Silence, and Peace; no boundary in any way. There won't even be the sense that 'I have to stay here' or 'I have to keep this'. The recognition will be, This Is. This alone is stable by itself – meaning, It does not require any other support.

The Self that you are, is already here, but recognition of this unchanging Space, this unchanging Awareness, must occur. For this reason, I ask you to recognise that which cannot leave. It cannot come and It cannot go, but within It there is taking place the play of comings and goings, watched in the presence of This.

What is being shared is not a teaching. It is only a reminder, an opportunity for recognition of what is already so. I'm not here to push you to develop, to create, to imagine, but point you back to what is eternally true. That alone which is perhaps deserving of the title: Constant.

It is unchanging, but if you make effort not to change, you cannot achieve it. Nobody can achieve it. Buddha did not achieve it, Jesus Christ did not achieve it, Krishna did not achieve it. You cannot achieve 'being still'. It is unachievable Stillness. It is natural; not acquired by any means. Presently, this is not clear for you because there is a fascination for movement – the movement of identity, the movement of doership – which somehow seems to eclipse this natural recognition of what is already here.

[*Silence*]

And not the movement by itself, but the belief in and the fascination for this movement causes blindness. It introduces amnesia in the Beingness. You are the Beingness. It is not a compliment that I am paying you. The point is: You are perfect!

But as long as your attention is rooted in the mind, this conviction will not be full. There will always be some doubt. Maybe you will have a glimpse, a flicker, but it will not stabilise, because you are holding onto the concepts of who you think you are, and you believe in your mind.

My feeling is, return to your country free. Whatever you carried here with you, leave it. The sacred fire of Arunachula is a good place to burn it. Go home empty. This will be the greatest gift to your nation, to your family, to your friends. Carry your passport, but you, be empty.

You are imagining that what you have studied
and what is inside your head is what you know.
But that is only what you think.
Only what is confirmed inside your Heart
is real Knowingness,
and the highest knowing and experience is:
'I am nothing'.

DEAD ON ARRIVAL

I can accept that life is constantly supporting me. I can begin to accept that I am already perfect and that things will come and go, but there is still a sense in me that I can prevent mistakes and pain.

Yes, this latter sense was evident from the very first statement you made, that you believe life is supporting you. My immediate response is, no, you *are* Life! There is not 'life' and 'you'. This statement, 'Life is looking after me' immediately arouses this response in me: You who?

As soon as you turn your attention away from your Self towards the experiential realm and regard it as the only reality, you end up feeling divorced from life. Separation enters your consciousness. Then somebody throws you a lifeline by introducing you to this question, 'Who am I?' If you dismiss it and instead try to satisfy yourself with just mental understanding, you will be dead on arrival.

It is deeply rooted in the psyche of humanity that we are separate from life; that there is both us and life.

"I've got a good life, have you got a good one?"

"Poor him, he's got a bad life."

But is it true? Is there one who can 'have life'?

You are Life!

If you cannot fully accept this, it is okay. Don't force acceptance, just allow this message enough space within to be heard, the possibility to be considered – that 'I am Life'. There's no gap between the unfolding of life and what you are. There is nothing other than you to point at to say this is 'my life'. There is nothing 'other' to report on.

The mind tries to convince you that this is not so. Functioning like an inner journalist, it constantly tries to catch up with what is unfolding. But any report it writes will always be past, and therefore an image of the truth, never the Truth itself. Even if the movement is a fraction of a nanosecond, you in whom the reported movement has already happened is faster, beyond fast. Because you contain the happening, it can only occur in You.

Your mind at present is trying to hide this Truth, it becomes anxious because conditioning arises inside the body still and it cannot be avoided. Consciousness is also acting this conditioning as it wakes up to the correct position within all of Its play.

Conditioning takes place in that area where conditioning can take place. But there is a place where conditioning cannot take place; from which the presence of conditioning, the effect of conditioning, and the play of conditioning is observed. You are that Seer. You are the passive Seer. You are not the active part. Who you really are is not interested in conditioning. In fact, ultimately, you don't even know anything called conditioning at all!

Who knows that joy
that arises when the question,
'Who am I?'
is asked and nothing is found?

PREGNANT WITH YOUR SELF

Ever since I've been on this spiritual journey, everything just keeps dropping away. I have no interest in anything. I feel like I've become very lazy. I can't keep any appointments. I can't commit to anything or do anything. Thoughts do come about the future, such as, how will I support myself without going after any work? I'm unsure if what is unfolding here is true or yet another avoidance game of the mind.

You are a rare case. You are pregnant with your Self. You are giving birth to your Self somehow. There comes a time when all interests fall away. Some people panic when this happens. They are afraid to be seen as uninteresting. But somehow you don't mind. In this phase of Self-discovery, some thoughts of the kind you have already mentioned may erupt from deep within the mind to scare you. They will try to cast a net of doubt over your spiritual evolution.

It is very close to me what you are sharing. It has been my experience as well that things were just falling away. I used to be a teacher at the local college in the middle of London. When the kiss from inside awoke in me this discovery of Self, the Heart directed me to quit my job. My own journey has taught me that in stripping down to pure Being, some experiences may appear in you that you would have never guessed had anything to do with you, but it feels so loud the moment it oozes out.

In my case, even though there had never been any interest in money, and this is true to this day, everything was leaving me to the point that I had nothing at all for a while. My last penny was spent; no more pennies were coming, and yet I knew in my heart that this was also part of the stage of purifying something. The experiences that came were part and parcel of a washing cycle to remove any remaining stains from the Beingness.

Some people say, "I have nothing", but they have five hundred pounds in the bank – that's their 'nothing' – but I mean I really had nothing! I was looking around in my pockets; I went through my old clothes to see if I could find some change or anything at all! There was no food and the belly started grumbling and I would turn to God, "It's time. It's time. Where are you?"

Sometimes doubts would arise to challenge this immense trust in God, who I regard as synonymous with Existence; they would suggest that God had abandoned me. But what outweighed these doubts was a feeling that something was revealing that 'I (God or Existence) am taking care of you'.

I remember my brother coming to visit me one day. He sat down and took out a stash of money and started counting. Here he was counting a bundle of money in front of me when I had none. A thought appeared then, 'If only I could have a pound I would be okay.' But inside I knew I was not to ask. It's the mind that wants it. It is the mind that fears not having the money and finds all sorts of justifications why it is okay to ask. I had given him money in the past and now would have been the perfect moment for the favour to be returned. But something even felt ashamed at the consideration to ask for anything and guided me to refrain. Following this higher calling, the mind kept on arguing, 'But this is a sign from God. He's telling you to ask your brother! Look how much money he has? This is your opportunity. Take it!'

But I'm telling you, it's not this. It doesn't show itself like this. It's like you have to be very quiet to be able to listen to pick out the voice of God from the noise of the mind. It's so intimate, this unseen Lover in you, who is now revealing all the tricks that you've been accustomed to and identified with. You get to see how skilled you've become. What a smooth operator you've been. All the little tricks, all the strategies, all the forcefulness that had been disguised as spontaneity are now being revealed for what they truly are. Yes, even what you used to call spontaneous was still forced, actually.

Everything is opened up to the light. You get to see that 'something' is afraid to hit rock bottom. If the initial fears that come are not allowed to tempt you to follow the counsel of the familiar mind, an immense feeling of Space and Freedom will be revealed to you. It's not what you'd expect. You'd expect to be desperate.

Someone like you is so blessed. All your little techniques and strategies for existing, all your 'street wiseness', have been combed out. Now you're like an infant again sitting in the lap of God. Let everything go. Rumi said something beautiful regarding this, 'Whoever brought me here must take me home.'

In each one of us a unique journey of discovery takes place. The mind is afraid to taste discomfort and will try to put obstacles in the way. It will try to deceive you with its cleverness. It will put philosophy in front of you. But you come to the fire with folded hands and with a firmness of heart not to enter any plea bargain. Just as you don't go to a restaurant carrying your own menu, you come to life like this: Let what comes, come. In that way all that is untrue is left behind and the Infinite is unveiled in Its magnificent splendour.

I'm very happy for you. I know the twists and turns of what has to happen when the Being is burping out all the lies. So it's very, very great. When relying upon your own skills has run you out of moves, in this moment everything becomes possible. When all the support has left you, you'll receive great surprises. Don't think that you know the way to your own deliverance.

When Life is kind enough to take everything from you, abundance in every way can come! Only now you are not depending anymore. You have ceased to be a beggar. Even abundance means nothing to you. Such is the path of the Free.

Don't imitate Ramana,
but follow his words
with trust and devotion
till you find yourself Home.

Walk by the light of your own Heart.
The flow of each river is unique.
I am beyond river and flow.
I am unbound Awareness.

BEING ASLEEP
WHILE FULLY AWAKE

I feel I am going crazy. When I do the enquiry, there are two that remain. There is me, the recogniser, and there is me I am recognising.

The 'I Am' that is witnessing all these things is one factor only. The tendency is for the identity to talk about the story of itself. But now the light has been turned onto that one for the first time ever. This one who has the story is what? Did you come to this point?

I see that I'm not the body but still I'm identifying myself with it.

Okay, give a little attention to that one that identifies with the body. Something is identifying itself with the body and that you call yourself. The identification with the body arises as a 'me' identity and says, 'I am doing this…'. That is also seen. So, the seeing of that must be happening at a deeper level.

There is the one that has a story about life: 'My name is George. I'm of this age and this nationality.' The body is not telling the story of George. But something is there holding the idea that 'I am the body'. This is thought. A thought arises,

'I am the body', and that thought arises as 'I'. This to you is the first identity. It is the body identity, and it feels intimate.

Let me tell you something, whatever says 'I' arises out of the Source. 'I' cannot come from anywhere else but the Source itself. Even the 'I' of the devil comes from that same Source.

What arises first out of the Source is the feeling 'I Am'. That 'I Am'-ness itself is called the Godly principle inside the form. All sentient beings have that feeling 'I Am'. It is pure in everybody. It is synonymous with Consciousness. Then the power to identify arises from this 'I Am'-ness with the instrument or the vehicle through which it is experiencing and tasting existence. This identification with the body also arises as 'I'. Unlike the primary 'I' that is pure, this secondary 'I' that is identified with the body is loaded with self-interest and conditioning. When this 'I' speaks, "I like, I prefer..., I, I, I, I", it carries with it a lot of psychological force and heaviness. It is this secondary 'I' you seem to identify with. Something is identifying with this 'I' which holds onto the 'I am the body' feeling. When it is strongly attached to the 'I am the body' feeling, then it arises as personality.

Imagine a swinging pendulum. Suppose the pendulum is your attention. On one end is the pure 'I Am'-ness feeling and on the other end is the 'I am me' or 'I am the body' feeling. When the pendulum swings to the 'I Am' end, there is just 'I Am'. The flavour of your experiencing is of spaciousness and stillness. There is joy and enjoyment of existence. Pleasure is in the Beingness. There is relaxation. There is peace. There is a natural flow of compassion to all that comes into your orbit. When the pendulum swings into 'I am me' – into time and who I am in identity – it is more noisy, strenuous, judging, threatened, attached, fearful, dreaming. When it swings again into the 'I Am'-ness, all of the noise is gone, and your experience is that of perceiving just like through your eyes alone. There is joy in this seeing. It is not personal.

Sri Nisargadatta Maharaj says it beautifully. He says:

> *The 'I Am'-ness is like a door*
> *that swings one way into all of manifestation*
> *and the other way into Infinity.*

This 'I Am'-ness is the same as Consciousness. But even the Consciousness comes and goes and is not stable. When the door in Maharaj's statement, which represents the 'I Am'-ness, is present, It perceives manifestation. You know this as the waking state. In the waking state, Consciousness is present and you're having the privilege of experiencing the potential of Consciousness to experience diversity. In deep sleep, Consciousness is gone. Consciousness is also called 'I Am', so 'I Am' is gone. The body is gone. But you are in total joy! When you are in the non-experiential state you are in complete joy! This is the state that Maharaj refers to with the door reaching Infinity. If you give it any consideration at all, you mistakenly believe that this non-experiential state is exclusive to the deep sleep state and disappears once the Consciousness and the waking state re-emerge together with experiences. Sri Nisargadatta does not say that the door must go. The import of his remark is that this Infinity is known by way of the 'I Am' itself. Because you give the dance of experiences on the screen of Consciousness your full attention, paying no attention whatsoever to the 'I Am' that is witnessing this play, you do not see this, and in turn you end up feeling miserable.

We are in love with the waking state, no doubt, but we also love the deep sleep state. In deep sleep you are totally in love but not in a dualistic sense, you are in the Unicity of Love. All beings love to be in that state where there is not even 'I'. And you love it, too!

As I was saying before, when the waking state comes over this pure state, you believe that this pure state has vanished, but I'm telling you, it is still here. These words you're hearing me speak are emanating out of this pure state. Sometimes this state is referred to as being asleep while fully awake.

This changefulness is also part of the Self, isn't it?

Everything is part of the Self. The changefulness is also part of the Self. You cannot distinguish the Self. You can only distinguish the appearances arising in the Self. But you've tied yourself to the appearances which are fleeting, so you feel unstable.

*The love you feel for a single being
could extend to include the whole world
without exhausting itself.*

SATSANG IS THE MIRROR
OF THE SELF

You say that the witness is apart and watches all that appears in Consciousness, but it seems to me that both the witness and the witnessed arise together and are therefore not separate.

This appears so, because you are speaking of the phenomenal or personal witness. The witness I point to is the pure Witness, which is impersonal and remains unaffected by either experience or the one who experiences. The pure Witness is beyond the mind and thus cannot arise in the mind. It is rather the other way around. The mind arises within the pure Witness. This personal witness you speak of is only another aspect of mind.

How can I become more fully established in that pure state?

It is impossible for 'you' to become established in It! From the outset you make the mistake in wrongly identifying yourself as an autonomous 'I' entity. This idea 'I' is only a thought appearing in and as mind. A thought cannot make effort to become 'no-thought', which is what your question implies.

'You' as an independent entity, are nothing but a concept. And you are suggesting that this concept can make an effort to become the Absolute, the effortless Reality. You can only be That. The pure state you speak of is your very Self. You are That! This understanding and recognition must be firmly established within. Then, you will know Truth spontaneously.

So there's nothing 'I' can do or need to do to be That? I am not sure if I feel completely hopeless or relieved by what you have just said.

Who feels relieved or hopeless? Please take a few moments right now and clarify this for yourself. Look within; trace the question back to where it is coming from. Don't be in any hurry. Start by being truly quiet and watch the inner response to this question. Again, who feels hopeless or relieved?

A strong sense of uneasiness is present somewhere inside my chest.

So a feeling is present inside and it is being interpreted as one of hopelessness. What happens if you don't identify with or judge the feeling, but instead just let the feeling be there? At the moment, you are pointing your attention towards the feeling and giving it importance. But now I ask you to bring the attention back to that which is aware of the feeling. Switch off the tendency to go outwards towards the experience. Remain only as the awareness itself.

Nothing is happening here.

Exactly! Nothing is happening. For happening to be experienced, you must go out into the region of the body-mind activity. Is there any sense of disappointment in response to this finding? Do you find that you are waiting for what happens next?

You have read my mind.

For 'next', mind is required. 'Next' suggests that attention is hunting for past, future, activities, feelings, thoughts and so on. All of this is seen and given reality with the mind. And mind, as intentional and non-intentional activity, is in turn also seen. Don't identify with the seen; be the ultimate Seer within which all of this takes place. Be careful not to make any image of this Seer either, as this too will be a creation of mind. See without interpretation and imagination, and there remains only Silence, only Space.

When I am in satsang . . .

This is also a thought. The moment you touch that thought, satsang comes into time and is held hostage by your mind. In truth, satsang is the mirror of the Self only. And when are you not your Self? Through habit, your attention, which Consciousness naturally identifies with, is constantly roaming about object-shopping and rarely rests in its Source. When attention goes out towards objects, such as thoughts and sensations, this is inattention. When attention remains in the Source, it is true attention. This attention will gradually merge and remain one with the Source and become synonymous with the Source, which is beyond both attention and inattention; It is nameless and formless. Be That!

Are you always in that state?

Yes, effortlessly and naturally I remain as That. But please understand, there is no entity to reach and remain in this natural state. You are already That. It is what we Are. Understanding this with pure mind and heart amounts to intimate seeing or direct experience and is all that is required. The rest is illusion. I tell you boldly because you entertain many doubts.

Doubts must also be illusion then.

Yes, and so is the doubter. [*Laughs*]

SEEING FROM FREEDOM

This Now which is present, which doesn't even know the concept of 'Now' and in which the concept of 'Now' arises in – it is the most fresh! So fresh, that there is no need to say 'Now', or 'Here'. Simply, the mind is being deconstructed of even the subtlest.

See from Silence! See from Emptiness! In the immediacy of your own understanding, you, as a separate entity, are undone. Then you are not seeing freedom, you are seeing from Freedom. You are Freedom. Phenomena can't entrap you.

There is an 'I' which arises from the mind and it always needs something. There is the 'I' intuition which arises out of Emptiness and is beyond need; it merely sees. And then there is that 'I'-less space within which the 'I' which is beyond need, is also perceived.

All this simultaneously, as One.

The concept is not Truth. It is not complete — not enough.
When the concept is swallowed inside your Heart,
concept becomes Presence — it becomes alive.
It becomes the creative energy of the Divine
and showers benevolence on the world.

MY FINAL QUESTION

Can you, the Perceiver, be seen? If I only had one question, I would ask you this, and I will keep asking you this. It is so potent a question that you could forget everything else you have ever heard or studied, and it would lead you Home.

If your existence is merely to satisfy your projections, to obtain comfort and objects, to acquire supernatural tricks, to find the 'perfect' relationship, or be successful in the material world then this question is not for you and I advise you to seek elsewhere. But if the fire is within you to discover your own Buddha-Nature, your own Christ-Consciousness or Krishna-Consciousness, your very own Self, then you cannot turn away from it. Everything is contained in this question. All else is secondary.

There is no need to try to feel at one with everyone, to experience the world as yourself, to love all. That may be revealed spontaneously, but don't work for it. Imposing a mental concept of 'oneness' on the world ultimately only nourishes the feeling of 'other'. It can cultivate arrogance in the shroud of false humility. To truly know the One underlying the whole of Creation, only this you need to do: Find out who you are, right now! Why waste time postponing this most precious of revelations?

Can you be the idea you have of yourself, your education, gender or nationality? That which is affected by the planets, can you be this? This discovery is available this very instant. Again I ask, can you, the Perceiver, be seen? Even on hearing this question, without the help of your mind, it is doing its work – a realignment of perception is happening.

Is there enjoyment for one who is free, you ask? Of course there is enjoyment. Enjoyment is not the monopoly of the mind or ego. Your entire Being is synonymous with joy.

At the lower levels of consciousness you need an object, a relationship, a goal, a concept, something other than you to enjoy and that is fine because this is also a kind of joy, though limited and transient. But at its truest and highest space, the Self is enjoying itself. It enjoys the manifestation of all without tying itself to any object or objective. This joy which is not about something, is the joy of the Free. And it cannot be compared, conveyed or imagined. It can only be experienced.

In fact, all the various flavours of joy you know and are hunting after are rooted in the one single joy of pure Being, including the present joy you experience of 'becoming'. How can any joy be separate when joy is the very nature of Existence? The difference between the joy of the Free and of the bound, is that the Free are not pursuing any 'thing' or any feeling, nor going to any sense of 'other' as 'other' is known experientially as oneself. So where is there to go, and what is there to chase? This inherent joy of the Free never passes.

We have learnt so many concepts which are not in service to the Truth that we are. This is all. It's a simple misunderstanding. When seen, what will be the outcome of this recognition? Unbroken silence and stillness. Unbroken joy. Such joy that even sorrow can appear in it and not eclipse it; where irritation, momentary anger, any emotion can arise but not linger. This joy encompasses the infinite potential and expression of Being.

Breaking through its own imagined constraints, unbroken joy, now, here, proclaims itself as You.

It is not important to be original;
it is important only to be true.

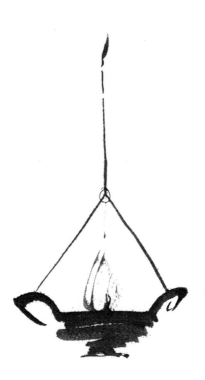

BREATH OF THE ABSOLUTE

In the Christian Bible, it says: 'In the beginning, God formed man from mud and water and then breathed life into him, and man became a living being.' So, which is man, the body or the breath?

Both. The vehicle for the spirit was formed from the earth. When it was completed, the Supreme Being breathed into the inert form and the inert form came to life. It began functioning as a biological body and thinking entity – a psychosomatic being – a wholeness. It is, here in the Bible, beautifully expressed. The breath of God is the life force, which announces itself in the feeling 'I Am' – the Consciousness – 'I exist'. Only then could the knowledge of being appear. Therefore, the sense 'I Am' is the breath of the Absolute.

But you say the Absolute is beyond the creative process.

Yes, though all manifestation springs forth from there only. First, Consciousness, the fluid Being, must manifest. It needs a body to announce Its presence and to express itself. When the body has been adequately prepared, the intelligent driver, the 'I Am'-Consciousness, along with the breath or life force, moves into position and the potential for harmonious and intelligent functioning is set into motion. Therefore, the Absolute, though not deliberately causing the manifest to appear, must be pointed to as the source of the appearance of all manifestation, though, It, itself is uncaused. Consciousness and the life force is, together, the breath of God. I'm taking the liberty here in referring to God as the Absolute.

From what position do you speak?

Pure understanding arises from the intellect of the manifest Absolute. It is the child (Consciousness) of God; the intuitive Knowingness of the universe appearing in the body of a human being.

In that case could you say you are God?

The 'I Am' is also God. Not in any separate or self-aggrandising sense, not personally, but as God is the only One, announcing Himself through the intuition or knowingness – 'I Am' – inside the body of each and every sentient being, none can exist apart from Him. The person has her being in God, for God is all-pervading – He is the single sentient Being. In India, the saying 'jiva is Shiva' finds an ease of acceptance. Here, 'jiva' refers to the individual and 'Shiva', the Supreme Being.

The term God brings up many uncomfortable connotations for me.

You may use the term Consciousness instead.

WHO IS MOOJI?

This has been my first experience of satsang. I have heard a lot of 'Who am I?' So my question is, who is Mooji?

Who is Mooji? [*laughs*]. Mooji is the expression, as each person is, of that which is infinite. The infinite Being expressing itself in each body, not only human bodies, but in every sentient being – this is what I am. It is felt inwardly as the sense 'I Am', 'I exist'. And this 'I' really means pure Consciousness. Somehow, this Consciousness identifies itself with the body which it needs to express and experience itself. The identification with the body is called Mooji or John or Susan.

Which country are you from? Maybe this isn't a pure Consciousness question, but it is something that many people would like to know.

For me, all of it is Consciousness. Even the person is Consciousness and so is the body. Everything that you see, hear, smell, feel and taste, I regard as forms of Consciousness. It's all-inclusive. But to come back to your question, where I am from, I am from Jamaica.

Were you acquainted with Jamaican spirituality?

Yes, it is impossible not to be. We are soaked in spirituality, if you want to call it that. Jamaica is primarily a Christian country. It is said that we have more churches or places of worship per square mile than anywhere else on earth. So we are very, very comfortable with the belief in God, and in having a relationship with God.

Apart from Christianity, is there also a spiritual connection with nature?

In Jamaica, we have an innate closeness to the land; there is no sense of it being separate. The power of nature is felt intuitively within, but not in some sophisticated way, just in a very natural way. What I am saying is that we were not aware of the concept of spirituality. I never even heard of this word 'spirituality' in Jamaica.

No, no. This is a new western way.

[*Mooji laughs*]

And then you moved to England. Why did you decide to go?

It was more like an acceptance of an invitation to come rather than a decision to go. My mother was already living in England. She had left Jamaica when I was a young child and so I didn't remember anything about her. When I was about fifteen, she started to write letters to me. I felt her coming back into my consciousness as if something inside was acknowledging a long lost truth as in 'I have a mother'. I welcomed this very deeply. When she actually came to see me, it was my first conscious meeting with her. She came with the intention of taking me back to England and introduced me to this idea of leaving Jamaica.

It must have been a big change, arriving in England. Did you feel comfortable with the way things were?

I had to adapt very quickly. I had to adapt to a different climate, a different culture, but at that age you take it in your stride.

The sunny climate of Jamaica obviously was not there in England, but did you find warmth in the people surrounding you at that time?

I was very lucky. When I arrived in London, it felt to me like I stepped into a warm embrace. My mother was part of the Seventh-day Adventist Church. The congregation represented a lovely support group. It was like being in the homely environment I had come from. The people were very friendly, welcoming, hugging and caring. It made things a lot easier.

When did you get introduced to the philosophy of Advaita?

That wasn't until 1993. But before that, in 1987, a big shift took place in the way I experience and perceive myself and life. It came about through a meeting I had with a man called Michael. In those days, I worked regularly as an artist making paintings, stained glass and sculptures. I came home one day and my girlfriend at that time said, "There was this young guy standing outside, looking at your stained glass in the window. He wants to meet you." He was guided to me somehow.

You had a feeling that he was guided to you?

Not immediately, but I came to see that. He was also an artist and as I was preparing an exhibition, I invited him to join, which he did. But he was very detached. It felt more like he was just supporting me in what I was doing.

One Sunday, he came by and we talked about God, faith, destiny, death and every other thing which I needed to get clarity on. There was a deep sense of peace and satisfaction. As he was leaving, I asked him, "Michael, when you pray again, will you pray for me?" "Well," he replied, "why don't we pray right now?" He was very direct and immediate in this way. I agreed, and he placed his hand on my shoulder and began praying. I don't remember what exactly he prayed, but as soon as he had finished, these words sprang from my mouth, "I am open to this, please help me." I often tell this story, because right there something happened inside me.

Can you describe what happened?

Well, immediately after this prayer, we hugged, then he said goodbye and left quietly. I felt especially happy. There was just a lovely feeling of happiness and warmth inside my heart.

Can you describe that especially happy feeling?

'Especially happy' means happy, not with excitement, but with peacefulness. Anyway, I felt tired so I went to bed early. When I awoke the next morning the sun was coming through a split in the curtains; a ray of sunlight with all those tiny dust flakes floating in it. It was like I had never seen the sun before. I thought to myself, 'Look at that!' I was looking at the sun and was feeling it inside me at the same time. It was beautiful.

You felt part of it?

It was an inner feeling of sweet joy, like I was really seeing for the first time – something fresh. There was a lovely sweetness about everything. I felt a lightness and softness inside my body and being, as if a dimmer switch of sensitivity was turned up to maximum. There was this tingling sensation, as if I were plugged into some mysterious electric realm. It was not shocking in any way; it was just a beautiful vibration inside. It felt very still and quiet. I remember all this distinctly. These feelings remained throughout the entire day and beyond.

Within a week of making that prayer with Michael, a deep peace arose inside my heart and it has never left.

Wow.

Yes, I never did anything for it. It was just there.

I think a lot of people long for that.

Yes. Yes. [*Silence*]

Then what happened?

Shortly after this, I started to go to the same church Michael was attending. It was just in the living room of somebody's house.

Was it a Christian church?

Yes, full of beloved young people. There was definitely something going on in that place. The energy was very intense; intense more than beautiful. People were speaking in tongues. I continued going there for a while. But after a short time I became uncomfortable with the style of the preaching at this church. It was very limited.

In what way was it limited?

There was a sectarian feeling; Christians against Muslims — some fundamentalist sentiments. If someone was not grounded or firm in their truth they could get indoctrinated. I was not attracted to that. I was already pulled inside the intimacy here [*pointing to chest*] and I related to it as God. I used to talk to God like we are talking now, casually. My experiences were contained in that. It was me and God and we live here, inside this body and heart. So I left this group. I felt some force took me away from them.

Besides Michael, was there another guide helping you?

No, the association with Michael led me to the Guide within.

When this Guide was revealed, I did not need any other guide. This inner force was revealing some very direct insights and experiences. For me they were miraculous, because I knew it had nothing to do with my cleverness, my previous experiences or any projection as I was completely fresh and new to all of this. The feeling was that I was being taken on some kind of inner journey. Then a lot started changing; inside and out. How I experienced the body, the clothes I wore, my hair, everything was changing.

Can you describe this a little?

I felt like growing my hair in locks. In my country, in those days, to grow your hair like this was a sign that you are stepping out of society.

Generally, your family won't be pleased with you, because there goes your career and future. So all this brought up some old personal memories, beliefs and conditioning, but the inner power held me firm.

Was there an outer as well as an inner power at work?

No, there is nothing outer for me. Everything was sprouting from that inner urge and I was just cooperating with that.

I also gave up my job and ended a struggling relationship.

You didn't have fears when you gave up your job?

No, it was a relief. There may have been some passing concerns, but already there was something here that was mightier than all those doubts – it made everything easier.

The satsangs you give are very much related to the Indian masters Ramana Maharshi and Papaji. How did you get acquainted with India?

Around this time, I read the entire Bible for the first time. I was not used to reading books. Up until then if I had a book with me, it was because it had pictures in it. I wasn't one for impressive words and any high thinking. After a while, there was a compulsion inside me to find out more about what was taking place. That's when I started to read. Shortly after I finished reading the Bible, I discovered a book about an Indian saint called Sri Ramakrishna. It was one of the first books I discovered from another culture. As I began reading about the life of this great saint, tears began flowing from me. I felt a huge relief. I was so happy. Sri Ramakrishna was a Hindu, a devotee of the Goddess Kali. His behaviour was very much in keeping with Hindu tradition: puja, mantras and ritual worship. But his language I found was completely universal. In this way, Ramakrishna gave me permission to accept what was arising inside spontaneously – the recognition that there is just the one Source, and all these differences were Its expression. I had felt this intuitively, but I needed to hear someone, a trusted authority, confirm what had announced itself inside my heart. Ramakrishna had this power.

Could you share it with anybody at the time?

Some of the experiences I tried to share with a few select

people, but it didn't work. It wasn't the time for that. Nobody could understand what I was experiencing. No one, not a single person could understand. I also found what was unfolding for me difficult to put into words. For a time, physically, I could not even speak.

Did you feel lonely then?

In those days, I had several friends who would visit but they would bring a social energy with them. Now something was turning away from that. I could not comfortably relate to them any longer. The old 'me' felt scooped out from inside and was replaced with a silent presence which needed no association. No matter how much 'I' tried, I couldn't connect with any voice that fixed me in the past anymore. This brought some momentary sadness. However, the power inside was so strong, that these sensations quickly vanished. I felt possessed by the Divine and loved every moment. There was little room for anything else. Sometimes, late at night, I would go out walking, often for several hours in the pitch darkness, completely charged with this beautiful, blissful presence.

Did you meditate at that time?

No, I didn't know anything about meditation. Sometimes I spent the entire night with the window open, looking out into the vacant sky. There were some big oak trees behind my house. I would often just sit in my little room, observing the leaves gently fluttering in the breeze. At other times there was a staring into the abyss of my inner Being. The whole universe was filled with effortless joy. Everything was joy. Going to sleep, there was joy; dreaming, there was joy; waking up, there was joy. Every action, there was joy! I couldn't get out of this joy or this peace. It and I were one – inseparable!

And still this is so?

Yes.

And then, you met Papaji?

Yes, I went to India in 1993 with the intention to go to Sri Ramakrishna's place, although he was not in the body anymore.

Where is that?

In Calcutta, a temple garden in Dakshineswar. I felt Ramakrishna's life story was so beautifully written up in *The Gospel of Sri Ramakrishna* and so atmospheric that I wanted to go there. But I never actually made it.

I came to India with no plans other than to visit Dakshineswar. Apart from clothing and a little bit of money, I brought nothing at all, not even a map. I went to Delhi first and after about ten days I was getting a bit bored. In my guesthouse I saw a sign 'Bus tours to Rishikesh'. The thought came, 'Ah, Rishikesh! That sounds like some holy place.' I left practically all my luggage in the hotel and went. I intended to spend the weekend there and then return to Delhi. But I did not return. Some six months later, a friend visiting the city on business, collected my belongings for me.

While in Rishikesh, I had a chance meeting with three devotees of Papaji's, who were just visiting for a night. I had never heard of Papaji or any contemporary Indian master. They kept on insisting, "You must meet Papaji! You must meet Papaji!" They invited me to travel with them to Lucknow where Papaji lived, but I was not ready. So they gave me the address and left. However, as soon as they had gone, I felt my time in Rishikesh was over. It was suddenly time to leave also. Instead of going straight to Lucknow, though, I went first to Varanasi, the holy city, for ten days.

Finally, in early November, 1993, I met Papaji.

[*Long silence*]

It was my first meeting with a guru.

But you met some gurus in Rishikesh, didn't you?

No, I saw many sadhus, but I didn't feel anything.

Did you immediately recognise Papaji as your own guru?

There was the recognition he was a master, but I did not feel he was my guru. And neither was I looking for one. I experienced God inside me as my father, guide and source; so the concept of requiring a 'guru' was not with me at the time. I didn't feel any particular connection with him. That came later. Nevertheless, I felt a natural awe in his presence like I had never experienced with another person. It was a surprise, the thrill moving inside my body in his presence.

Before we go further with that, can you explain a little more about some of this Indian terminology, and how Ramakrishna, Papaji and Ramana Maharshi are connected? Many people don't know very much about them.

Generally, most of the people you see dressed in orange in India are called sadhus. They are monks, and they usually move about from town to town, or to and from holy sites depending on the weather and the spiritual calendar of the year. Then, there are those who are called saints. They have realised God in some form, and most are devotional in their background and temperament. And then there is what is called a 'jnani', a fully Self-realised being who has transcended the ego identification.

Sri Ramakrishna is a Jnani and at the same time, he is a great devotee, or Bhakta, of Goddess Kali. There are many followers of Sri Ramakrishna in India.

Sri Poonja or Papaji is regarded as a living Buddha, a Jnani or fully awakened Master of Truth. He also has a background of devotion. His own Guru is Sri Ramana Maharshi. We are in the vicinity of Ramana here, in Tiruvannamalai. This mountain you see before us is the holy mountain, Arunachala, and is considered the embodiment of Lord Shiva Himself, the Supreme Consciousness in Hinduism. It is also very much associated with Ramana Maharshi. Tiruvannamalai is one of the most important places in India for followers of Advaita Vedanta, which is the philosophy or the path of non-duality. The philosophy of non-duality conveys as best as can be done with words, the Truth as it is alive in those who have realised It. What they experience is that all is emanating out of one

Reality and that they themselves are one with That.

Advaita was the theory for what you had been feeling already?

No, initially during my time in London, even though God was felt inside me and there was the intuition that there was only one God but many expressions, there was still the sense of me and God. That feeling is still present today, but the sense of Oneness is also there. Both perspectives are there together against a background of pure, unmoving Awareness. There is the seeing and understanding appearing in Emptiness. Sometimes I have the feeling that I am God's servant or God's devotee, and at other times I feel there is no separation at all. There is just a constant joyful feeling inside.

When you met Papaji and were introduced to Advaita, did you read anymore then?

Following the first kiss from within, I read a little bit, but when I met Papaji, the energy to read wasn't strong. The words pouring out from him, from his own mouth, were more forceful than any words on a page. These living words were enough, they had power.

Was Papaji expecting you when you arrived?

He wasn't expecting me personally. [*Laughs*]

Sometimes you hear these stories of people saying, "He was expecting me. He knew I was coming!"

Yes, sometimes people would come to Papaji and they would have a feeling that Papaji was going to recognise them and say, "Aha, you have come!" But he would just ignore them; their egos got completely crushed.

So he did recognise them?

Well he recognised their ego! Slap! [*Laughs*]

And your ego?

Oh yes, definitely.

Did he recognise your ego?

No, no. To be exact he doesn't see any egos, but egos are bursting in his presence. To see an ego, you have to be an ego. His eyes are not so low to see egos. His eyes are clean so he cannot see ego.

But Papaji died, right?

No, Papaji doesn't die.

He went out of his body.

Somebody once asked me, "When did your Master die?" I said, "The Master never dies; it is the mister that dies, but the Master, that principle, can never die." Papaji as I know him in my heart is the same as my own Self or your own Self – the

Formless. I know many people don't understand this. They think, 'Of course he died. His body is not here anymore.' This is nonsense! You never die. You cannot die. Nobody dies. Nobody ever dies.

And how much time did you spend with Papaji?

Not that long, the first time in 1993, maybe four and a half to five months. Then I came here to Tiruvannamalai for the first time in 1994 and spent two months near Ramana's Ashram before going back to be with Papaji again just for a couple of weeks or so. I last saw Papaji in the body in 1997. I stayed with him for another four to four and a half months. A month after I returned to London he left his frame.

And what happened in that time with Papaji?

Well before I met Papaji, I was nearly in a constant space of blissfulness, of joy, of miracles. But it was not always so smooth, sometimes the ego would come up, it could be very nasty, and then again this wonderful power would wash all miseries away.

Ever since that first encounter with Michael when we both prayed together, my experience of phenomena had become more subtle. The material world wasn't just bricks and stones, rocks and water anymore. I perceived the whole world energetically. But when I met Papaji, the feeling of Emptiness began. My mind was emptying from these worldly references. They were insignificant. There was a still joy and peace, but the connections were fading. The stories were dying.

So when did you realise Papaji was your guru?

The recognition came on the day that I sat at his feet in satsang, whilst he read my letter openly for all to hear. My body had been trembling before I went up, but even so, my reactions were startling. Papaji was responding to my letter when a sudden rage arose within me. It was totally out of the blue. I felt insulted, misunderstood and ridiculed in front of everyone, despite the fact that I could not actually hear what he was saying! There was a loud ringing inside my head which blotted out his voice. I just wanted to leave. I didn't like him in that moment, not in the least. My mind was rebelling, 'You are not my guru. I don't accept your advice. Only a master like Ramana will I prostrate to.' The only words from Papaji that filtered through this deafening anger were, "For surrender to be complete, you must completely disappear." In that instant, I rejected any idea of him being my guru.

After satsang, I decided to leave Lucknow for good. I felt this shake up was just what I needed to get a move on. It was a very hot day, so I took a break from packing my things to go for a walk to the nearby shopping area. I sat down under a tree, still very upset at what had happened earlier. After half an hour or so, I got up and headed in the direction for home. For twenty or so steps I was still immersed in this agitated state of feeling lost. Then the next step! It was as if a dark, heavy cloud lifted, taking with it everything inside my head. There was nothing! I could not find any reference for myself. I could not find myself or any 'self' at all! There was only Emptiness. Of course, I could see my body, my hands, particularly for some reason my palms, but they had nothing to do with a 'self', they didn't belong to me. There was no memory, no time, no meaningful connections. I could not find anything that felt like, 'Okay, this at least exists'. Nothing existed. There was only incredible space and infinite silence.

After some minutes, a quarter of an hour at most, I felt Papaji's presence filling in everywhere but not separate from what I am. Then, for the first time, I felt enormous love for Papaji. In that moment I met my Master. [*Silence*]

I started running towards his house immediately, which was nearly a mile away. My feet felt as though they were not touching the ground; it was completely effortless. There was great peace and at the same time a strange excitement flowed through my veins, yet inwardly, nothing was actually 'happening'.

I don't remember anything after this. It was as if my mind stopped recording in the name of my ego. It's been like this ever since.

Did you ever talk with Papaji about this?

No, he knew.

Do not remind the world
it is bound or suffering.

Remind the world
it is beautiful and free.

A NOTE ON ARUNACHALA

'Om Arunachaleswaraya Namaha'

For thousands of years, sages, saints and seekers of the Truth have gathered at Arunachala, near which is situated the Southern Indian town of Tiruvannamalai, in Tamil Nadu. The first mention of this mountain is found in the Rig Veda, in the passage narrating the mighty battle between Vishnu and Brahma to decide who was the greater. Shiva, disgusted by this display of delusion and ego, manifested as a column of Light without beginning or end, to show that He alone was the Supreme Lord. Vishnu, humbled by this display of omnipotence, requested that Shiva, as this column of Light, be made manifest as a lingam (symbol of the Supreme Absolute) on earth. And thus, Arunachala came into being.

In the *Arunachala Mahatmyam* (from the Skanda Purana), it is said that this hill is so sacred that merely thinking of it brings one to realisation of the Truth. In the same text it is stated that whereas Kailas is the abode of Shiva, Arunachala is the embodiment of Shiva Himself, Wisdom manifest, and this is a great secret – in that only those who thirst for Liberation will hear of It. This explains why, despite its renown amongst followers of Advaita Vedanta, and compared to other

Shiva pilgrimage sites, it has remained largely unknown.

Sri Ramana Maharshi, through His devotion and love of the mountain as Self, His translation of the sacred scriptures, and in the composition of His own writings and songs dedicated to Arunachala, is considered responsible for bringing news of this Divine manifestation to the general public, and to the West. His own transmission of the Truth, like the mountain, was made through silent Presence. He said of His beloved Sadguru, 'Only to reveal Your state without speech, You stand as a hill shining from earth to sky.'

ACKNOWLEDGEMENTS

Mooji and the editors wish to extend their infinite gratitude to the many friends who assisted in compiling these dialogues.

No editing would ever occur if it weren't for the steady commitment of Gayatri, Hari Dharma, Nataraaj, Omkara and Mirabai who record Mooji's satsangs in both audio and video formats, and who give so much of their time, energy and love in enabling satsang to reach people all over the world.

Producing a good transcript, which forms the basis of this type of editing work, requires great skill and attention. For their loving contribution, we wish to extend a heartfelt thank you to Christina Kohlboeck (Samani), Shanna Paice, Celia Teresita Freidenberg (Shanti), Sundaram Hammond and Tania Gerich, and to Daya Doris Hargrave for her additional editing.

We are greatly indebted to Priya and Sri who are excellent administrators and support in ways too numerous to recount here and whose joy in doing so is contagious.

Nataraaj deserves credit for proofreading the manuscript and for giving us valuable suggestions for improvements. Likewise, John Arnold is thanked for his keen eye and feedback.

Special thanks go to Gayatri for her patient scanning of Mooji's drawings and to Jyoti for not only applying her magic wand so that the pictures were usable in print, but also for creating a design concept alongside Mooji as a basis for this beautiful book cover, and for burning the midnight candle on more than one occasion. Satyadevi, Tara, Shankari and Hari Dharma must also be recognised for their help as creative midwives in easing the process.

Deep gratitude to Gautam Sachdeva, and his team at Yogi Impressions, for their skill and hard work in producing a book of exceptional quality under the pressures of an extremely tight deadline, and for being such a pleasure to work with. In particular, alongside Gautam, we thank Girish Jathar for his technical support without which a manuscript wouldn't have emerged for Sanjay Malandkar to lay out into appealing and readable pages; Priya Mehta for her dynamic vision and application in taking what was a design concept into its final brilliance as a book cover; and to Shiv Sharma for ironing out the editing and resolving those small but essential points of language which baffle the majority of us.

We acknowledge that 'Who Is Mooji?' and 'Advaita – The Pathless Path' were adapted from an interview Mooji gave years ago at Arunachala. Saskia Beugel of Rishis' Club for Free Souls, Amsterdam, Holland, was the interviewer.

And finally, to all those wonderful people who attended and participated in satsang at the foot of the sacred mountain, without you, Mooji's wisdom would not have graced these pages at all.

With Love. Om Shanti, Shanti, Shanti . . .

Further details about Mooji's work and schedule
are available at the website
www.mooji.org

For information about Mooji's previous book, *Before I Am,*
and satsang recordings in audio and DVD formats,
you are welcome to visit
www.mooji.org/shop/

Mooji is also on YouTube
www.youtube.com/user/moojiji

For further details, contact:
Yogi Impressions Books Pvt. Ltd.
1711, Centre 1, World Trade Centre,
Cuffe Parade, Mumbai 400 005, India.

Fill in the Mailing List form on our website
and receive, via email, information on
books, authors, events and more.
Visit: www.yogiimpressions.com

Telephone: (022) 22155036/7/8
Fax: (022) 22155039
E-mail: yogi@yogiimpressions.com

Also visit:
indiayōgi.
www.indiayogi.com

the complete spiritual e-shop

Breinigsville, PA USA
29 July 2010
242708BV00003B/32/P